BLESSED COLUMBA MARMION

To the affectionate memory of
Benoît Becker and Gisbert Ghysens
Monks of Maredsous,
and
Bernard O'Dea
Monk of Glenstal

Mark Tierney OSB

Blessed
Columba
Marmion

A SHORT BIOGRAPHY

A Liturgical Press Book

THE LITURGICAL PRESS
Collegeville, Minnesota
www.litpress.org

Published in the United States of America and Canada by
The Liturgical Press,
Collegeville, Minnesota 56321
in association with The Columba Press, Dublin, Ireland

Cover by Bill Bolger
Origination by The Columba Press
Printed in Ireland by
Colour Books Ltd, Dublin

ISBN 0-8146-2756-0

Table of Contents

Columba Marmion in 1914

Preface

My previous work on Marmion, *Columba Marmion: A biography*, appeared in 1994. At that time, the process for the cause of his beatification had already been introduced to Rome. Such a process is a slow affair and takes many years of research and decision-making. Then, quite suddenly, on 5 February 2000, it was announced that Pope John Paul II had decided to beatify Marmion on 3 September 2000. Two final requirements had evidently been fulfilled to allow this to happen. First of all, on 28 June 1999, the decree regarding Columba Marmion's practice of heroic virtue throughout his life was promulgated. And secondly, on 27 January 2000, the decree attesting that a miracle of healing, performed through the intercession of Marmion, had been approved by Pope John Paul II. The miracle in question related to the cure from terminal cancer of a woman from St Cloud, Minnesota, USA. She had been given three months to live when, in August 1966, she and her husband visited the Abbey of Maredsous in Belgium, and prayed at the tomb of Abbot Columba Marmion. On her return to the USA it was discovered that all signs of cancer had disappeared. She has now been cancer free for 34 years and leads a happy and productive life as a mother and grandmother. In a recent interview this woman, Mrs Patricia Bitzan, said: 'I'm just a tool. The miracle was a gift to me, but it was not because I was so wonderful. I don't know what to say, really, except that I'm very grateful for what happened to me. I've been touched by a saint, or a future saint.'

Columba Marmion was undoubtedly an extraordinary man, whose life has touched many people. He is best known through his writings. Three of his books have become spiritual classics, *Christ, the life of the soul, Christ, in his Mysteries,* and *Christ, the ideal of the monk,* and have been translated into sixteen languages, including Korean and Japanese. Born in the middle of the nineteenth century, of an Irish father and French mother, he became very much a twentieth-century European. His spiritual message is equally valid in this twenty-first century. Marmion (1858-1923) was a Dubliner, and while he left Ireland to live in Belgium when he was twenty-eight, he remained Irish at heart and visited Ireland as often as possible. It is said that he never lost his Irish accent.

His name lives on to this day in many places. He is particularly remembered in the Abbey of Maredsous, Belgium, where he was Abbot from 1909-1923 and where his body rests in the chapel of St Gregory the Great in the Abbey church. It comes as a surprise to many to learn that there is a Benedictine monastery in Aurora, Illinois, USA, called Marmion Abbey, founded in memory of him in 1933, only ten years after his death. Marmion Bridge, over the River Slaney, near Enniscorthy, is called after him. In Dundrum, Co Dublin, where Marmion served as curate in 1881 and 1882, there is a large Day-Care Centre, called Marmion House, run by a voluntary group called the Marmion Society. There is a housing estate near Arran Quay in Dublin, where Marmion was born, called Marmion Court. Such instances could be multiplied. He is certainly not entirely forgotten in the country of his origin. The story of his life deserves to be told and read, not only in Ireland but also in the USA, in Belgium, and throughout Europe. Though Irish by birth, he became a European by adoption, as well as by choice. He is, incidentally, the first Irish Benedictine monk ever to be beatified.

Mark Tierney,
Glenstal Abbey,
Murroe,
Co Limerick,
Ireland.
5 July 2000

Prologue

The young, newly ordained, Irish priest was making his way back to Ireland from Rome in the summer of 1881. He had decided, en route, to visit the Benedictine Abbey of Maredsous, in Belgium, to see another newly ordained priest, L'Abbé Moreau, a contemporary of his in Rome, who had entered the novitiate in Maredsous earlier that summer. Thus on 23 July 1881, the Irish priest found himself descending from the train at a placed called Yvoir, the railway station nearest to the Abbey of Maredsous. It was about eight miles from the monastery, and there were no buses, or taxis, or their equivalent, to be had. Thus, with his two suit-cases, one in each hand, he began the long walk to the monastery.

It was high summer, very hot, and he was wearing his clerical collar and black suit. Fortunately, just outside Yvoir, he met a kind Belgian countryman, who happened to be going his way and who offered to carry one of the suit-cases and accompany him as far as Maredsous. The man spoke the local dialect, Walloon, a very old Frankish tongue, composed mainly of French and Latin words. However they managed to converse, as the young priest was half-French, and a fluent Latin speaker. The Belgian produced some sandwiches, which he shared with the priest, and the latter paid for a drink at a wayside inn.

It was evening before they arrived at Maredsous. The young Irish priest then said goodbye to his friend, and proceeded to knock at the door of the monastery. On entering, he was immediately impressed by the peace and silence of the vast cloisters of the abbey, and felt transported back to the eleventh or twelfth century. Indeed, he was quite overwhelmed by the reception given him by the Abbot, Dom Placide Wolter, and the community of Maredsous. This visit was to be a turning-point in the life of the young Irish priest. He quite suddenly realised that he, like his friend, Moreau, had been called by God to become a Benedictine monk in this monastery of Maredsous.

However, he was not a free agent at this time, being a diocesan priest from Dublin, and under orders from his archbishop, Dr McCabe, to proceed to his first parish assignment in Dundrum, Co Dublin. Thus, after spending two memorable days in Maredsous, the Irish priest, whose name was Father Joseph Marmion, left for Ireland. Somehow he knew in his heart that he would return to Belgium and join this newly founded Belgian monastery. He could not possibly have foreseen that, one day, he would become the Abbot of Maredsous, and one of the best-known and best-loved figures in Ireland, England, Belgium and throughout the Catholic world. This visit to Maredsous was not his first walk with destiny, but it was the most significant one in his life.

Part I

The Marmion family c. 1864. Joseph, dressed in black, is fifth from the left.

CHAPTER 1

The Early Years (1858-1873)

Family Background

Joseph Marmion, the future Abbot Columba Marmion, was born in Dublin on 1 April 1858, the son of William Marmion and his wife, Herminie Cordier. The Marmions were of Norman origin and are found in Ireland from the beginning of the thirteenth century. Robert de Marmion (The Justice), was in Ireland in 1210, serving under King John. His youngest son, Gilbert, remained in Ireland, and was the progenitor of the Irish branch of the family. The immediate ancestors of Joseph Marmion came from the borders of Counties Meath and Kildare. His paternal grandfather, Matthew Marmion, was born at Woodlands, Kilmessan, Co Meath, in 1790, and married Elizabeth Rourke, from Clane, Co Kildare, in 1818. The couple went to live in Clane, where Elizabeth's family had a house and farm, which she inherited. They had three children, William, Matthew and Rose. William was the father of Joseph Marmion.

Sometime in the 1840s, William Marmion decided to take up a business career and moved to Dublin. He lived at 57 Queen Street, working as a salesman in the firm of Vernon and Cullen, Corn-Factors, on Arran Quay. In 1847 he met his future wife, Herminie Cordier, a French lady, who was spending some time in Dublin learning English. According to a family tradition, they fell in love at first sight. The marriage ceremony was celebrated in the church of St Andrew, Westland Row, Dublin, on 21 April 1847. At the time of his marriage, William Marmion was quite prosperous, with an annual salary of £500. However, he was scrupulously religious, and since Herminie did not have her certificate of baptism with her in Ireland, he insisted on her being conditionally baptised on the eve of the wedding. From all the evidence available, it seems that William Marmion was a rather straight-laced sort of person, who, according to a close friend of the family 'possessed a rather Victorian-type character, pompous, solemn and even authoritarian'. Herminie, on the other hand, was docile and less assertive than her husband. Certainly, husband and wife were quite different as regards their individual personalities, but they provided a stable and happy home for their children. We never hear of any tensions or problems in the family circle. Security and contentment were the key-notes of young Joseph Marmion's upbringing.

Nine children were born to William and Herminie, four girls and five boys. Joseph was the seventh child and third boy. The first two boys had died in infancy, and thus the parents had a special reason for rejoicing when they had this third son, whom they cared for with extra attention. The following are the children in order of birth:

Mary	Born 1 May 1848
Lizzie	Born 27 April 1849
John	Died aged 2 years
Philip	Died aged 1 year
Flora	Born 29 June 1853
Rose	Born 1 February 1855
Joseph	Born 1 April 1858
Frank	Born 4 October 1860
Matthew	Born 24 October 1863

Childhood and youth of Joseph Marmion

Before his birth, his parents had prayed to St Joseph for a son, and in thanksgiving, decided to call him Joseph. Thus, when on 6 April 1858, five days after his birth, he was baptised in the church of St Paul, Arran Quay, Dublin, he received the names Joseph Aloysius. William and Herminie Marmion, both religious people, looked upon their son as a special blessing, and in their hearts had already dedicated him to God. Even at this early stage, they took it for granted that he would become a priest, and planned his future with this in mind. As soon as he was old enough to wear boy's clothes, they dressed him in black, and he continued to wear black clothes all the time he was under his parents' roof. On the other hand, the rest of the Marmion children were dressed in varying colours, as can be seen from an early family photograph, taken in 1864. As a child, Joseph was not very robust, being subject to bouts of asthma. Several times his life was despaired of, but by the age of eight he had grown stronger and lost all traces of his earlier poor health.

During these early years of his life, Joseph Marmion came under the influence of his aunt, Miss Kate O'Sullivan, a very pious lady, and half-sister to his father. Kate lived with the Marmion family in Dublin, somewhat in the capacity of an au pair or nanny, and took a special interest in young Joseph. By 1863, the family had moved to 2 Blackhall Place, just around the corner from 57 Queen Street. William Marmion had found a new and more lucrative position, as director in the firm of Branigan and Bryson, corn-importers, at Smithfield, Dublin. Herminie, Joseph's mother, gave private lessons in French to students, and for some time was employed as French governess to the Vice-Regal household. We also hear of young Joseph going on holidays to his cousins in Clane, Co Kildare, and of his visiting the chapel in Clongowes Wood nearby to say his prayers.

Joseph Marmion received his first formal education in a primary school called St Laurence O'Toole's School, run by the Augustinian Fathers of John's Lane, not far from the Marmion home. After less than a year at this school, he transferred on 11 January 1869 to Belvedere College, where he began his secondary education. Belvedere was run by the Jesuits, and the headmaster, or rector, at the time was Father Edward Kelly. By all accounts he was an outstanding priest and educator. At any rate, Joseph Marmion received an excellent grounding in Greek and Latin, and also learned the art of public speaking in the school Debating Society. The students of Belvedere College did not wear any distinctive school uniform, and Joseph, because of his black clothes, had to overcome the ridicule of his classmates. Fortunately he excelled in his studies to such a degree that he became the object of envy, rather than of scorn, to others. He always retained happy memories of his time in Belvedere, where he clearly proved himself above the average in intelligence and maturity. When only fifteen years and nine months old, he successfully passed a scholarship examination, entitling him to a place in Holy Cross College, Clonliffe, the Dublin Diocesan Seminary.

According to his own account, written many years later, he was approached by the Jesuits, while still a pupil at Belvedere, suggesting that he might enter the Company of Jesus. He had an interview with the Father Provincial, and seriously considered this option. However, at the same time other influences were at work on his young mind, and he finally opted for the secular clergy. He explained his decision in the following words: 'on account of the shortage of diocesan priests, Cardinal Cullen, the Archbishop of Dublin, discouraged me from following my own desires'. In the light of his future entering monastic life, it is interesting to note that already, at this early age, he seriously thought of joining a religious order. And, as far as we know, he never completely put the idea out of his mind.

CHAPTER 2

The Long Road to the Cloister
(1874-1886)

Student at Holy Cross College, Clonliffe, 1874-1879
Holy Cross College, Clonliffe, was founded in 1859 by Archbishop Paul Cullen, as a seminary for future priests of the
Dublin diocese. Situated in Drumcondra, in north Dublin, and
within ten minutes walk from the city centre, it has spacious,
well-kept grounds. The buildings, recently constructed, which
included a Roman-style church, were more than adequate for
the eighty or so students who were housed there in 1874. The
president of the college at the time was an outstanding priest, Dr
Michael Verdon. A man of high principle and of amiable character, he knew how to set high standards and get the best out of his
students. He had a profound influence on the young Marmion,
and remained a life-long friend. Another priest on the staff in
Clonliffe, and dean of the college from 1874-1879, was Fr
Bartholomew Fitzpatrick, who also became a close friend of
Joseph Marmion. However, the priest who undoubtedly exercised the most influence on the spiritual life of Marmion during
his years in Clonliffe was Fr John Gowan CM. By the time
Joseph Marmion entered Clonliffe in 1874, Fr Gowan had been
spiritual director of the students for twenty years. He was both
strict and exacting, and a good judge of character. This was an
age when spiritual direction was an accepted part of a seminari-
an's training. Certainly Fr Gowan was not afraid to try their
spirits, and proposed a rigid discipline for the students. He gave
a weekly conference, during which he imparted to them his own
devotion to the Passion of Jesus Christ, recommending the daily
round of the Stations of the Cross. It was at the suggestion of Fr
Gowan that Marmion made a pact of silence with some of his
fellow students, and found the practice very helpful for recollection. It was also during his time in Clonliffe, that he had his first
mystical experience. One day, coming out of the lecture-hall, he

was privileged to receive a special grace – a divine illumination.
It lasted only a few seconds, and consisted of a vision of the
Infinity of God. He was led to make an immediate Act of
Adoration, and remembered this moment for the rest of his life.
Towards the end of his time in Clonliffe, Marmion made a pact
or promise with two of his fellow-students. Dated March 1879, it
had undoubtedly been inspired by something he had read in the
life of Blessed John Berchmans. It was duly signed by all three
students, Joseph A. Marmion, Patrick P. Hannigan and James J.
Dunne, and authorized by their confessor. It bound all three to
daily prayer, plus acts for three intentions: tender devotion to
the Mother of God, profound humility, and ardent love for
souls. Marmion referred to this 'promise', in a letter to his friend
Patrick V. Dwyer, in 1890:

> I never forget the promise which we made (James Dunne,
> you and I) and I am faithful to the little practices which we
> undertook. Sometimes I think what a joy it will be for us to
> find, after a few years, that we have contributed to save each
> other's souls. I feel that God will bless, by a closer union of
> our hearts in heaven, the spiritual union commenced for His
> love here on earth.

Marmion's six years in Clonliffe were very important for both
his intellectual and spiritual development. He approached the
study of philosophy and theology in a supernatural spirit, in
order to deepen his own piety and love of God. Although very
young in years, he possessed the necessary maturity of mind to
seek holiness 'here and now' as a student, in order to be a good
priest when the time came for him to be ordained. It was a com-
bination of prudence and foresight, as well as a genuine inner
urging of the spirit of God, which helped him maintain a high
standard of life as a student. However, it was not all plain-sail-
ing. He explained one problem which he had to face, and which
was solved for him through prayer:

> When I had finished my course of Philosophy, I was inclined
> to think of God rather as a tyrant. But one day, as I was pray-
> ing at the foot of the Cross, Our Lord seemed to say to me:
> 'No greater love can a man have'. And then He seemed to
> add: 'I and the Father are One. That love of mine is a reflec-
> tion of My Father.' From that moment on, I always visualised
> God as Love.

One other essential factor must be mentioned regarding these Clonliffe days, as it was to become a life-long characteristic of Marmion: his ability to make friends and to maintain friendships. The old saying: 'Know me, know my friends,' was especially true of the young Marmion. Perhaps he was lucky in his contemporaries at Clonliffe. These may have been 'vintage years' for the college, with an extra special crop of excellent and talented young men. Be that as it may, it all helped Marmion to develop this emotional and sensitive side of his character. He found in these relationships an opportunity to share and give himself to others, which was closely akin to giving himself to God. From his early days, he had an extraordinary 'openness' vis-à-vis people. He had a large and open heart, and saw people as instruments of grace, not as obstacles to sanctity. Thus, during these years, he worked out a theology of friendship and fellowship, which provided a strong spiritual bond and support. These were no mere passing or sentimental relationships but were seen in a spiritual context.

From time to time, throughout his later years in Clonliffe, Marmion found himself tempted to join some religious order. One of his contemporaries gave the following account of these vocational doubts:

> Joseph Marmion always seemed to have a leaning to religious life. I am sure nearly every religious who gave a retreat to the students in Clonliffe inspired him with the desire to join his Order or Congregation. On one occasion, a passing visit to a House of Passionists seemed likely to determine him to become a Passionist. However, the Spiritual Director of his time, Fr John Gowan, must have exercised a great steadying influence on him, whilst in no way abating his fervour.

Such problems and doubts often come to seminarians, especially to those who, like Marmion, were continually seeking the way of perfection, and who were at the same time somewhat impressionable. Evidently, it did not cause him too much trouble, though he never entirely banished the idea from his head. Two events probably led to the temporary abandonment of any idea of entering a religious order. The first was the death of his father on 9 April 1878, aged only 58 years. Joseph Marmion was now the head of the family, and he had to assume new responsibilities, *vis-à-vis* his mother and two younger brothers, Frank and Matthew. The family were in reduced financial circumstances after the death of the father.

Joseph Marmion's success as a theological student in Clonliffe, is evidenced by the fact that he carried off most of the prizes in the summer examinations of 1879. He excelled in the following subjects on the curriculum: Biblical Studies, Dogma, Moral, Canon Law, Church History and Sacred Liturgy. It must have come as no surprise to him when, in the autumn of 1879, he was told by his superiors that he had been chosen to complete his theological studies in Rome, and that he would be leaving Clonliffe before Christmas of that year. The recently appointed Archbishop of Dublin, Dr Edward McCabe, acting on the advice of the President of Clonliffe College, was responsible for this choice of Marmion as a candidate for further studies in Rome. This appointment was both an honour and a privilege, not conferred on every student, and is a further indication of the high intellectual qualities and good moral record of Joseph Marmion. The decision meant that he would be absent from Dublin – and from his family – for at least two years. The thought of having to leave his widowed mother and two younger brothers for two years must have been a considerable sacrifice for Joseph Marmion. It was also to be his first experience of living abroad as an exile. However, he accepted the decision of his archbishop and superiors without demur, believing that he was acting under obedience. He was to lodge in the Irish College, Rome, while studying theology at the College of Propaganda.

Rome, December 1879-July 1881
Some time before Christmas 1879, Marmion travelled to Rome in the company of the former President of Clonliffe, Dr Michael Verdon, who was about to take up his post as Vice-Rector of the Irish College, Rome. Dr Verdon became ill when the boat reached Marseilles, and stayed in the South of France to recuperate. Marmion, however, proceeded on his journey and arrived in Rome on 24 December 1879. He was warmly greeted by the Rector of the Irish College, Mgr Tobias Kirby who was an extremely pious and worthy priest, with a shrewd understanding of character. He immediately recognised the talents of Joseph Marmion, and later took him as his private secretary. Indeed, these eighteen months in Rome were to prove a very fruitful

time for Marmion. He later declared that 'my stay in Rome was the happiest period of my life.' He was able to deepen his understanding of theology and sacred scripture, which formed an essential basis for his future preaching and writing. It was also during his study in Italy that he first felt the call to the Benedictine way of life. Marmion was very fortunate in having a group of eminent professors at the College of Propaganda Fide. The most important of these was the Abbé Francis Satolli, a leading Thomist scholar, who encouraged the young Marmion to throw himself into a study of the *Summa* of St Thomas Aquinas. On several occasions, Marmion was invited by Satolli to come to the rostrum and defend one or other theological thesis. According to a contemporary of Marmion at Propaganda College, Joseph Moreau:

> ... there would follow complete silence, while all the students listened in admiration, as Marmion, with a surety and clarity, showing that he was master of his subject, dealt with the question asked. At the end of such a demonstration, Joseph Marmion often received the warm congratulations of the professor and the students.

Marmion was given Minor Orders in Rome on 27 February 1881, in the Irish College. He received the Subdiaconate on 12 March 1881 and the Diaconate on 16 April 1881, both at the hands of Mgr Julius Lenti, in the Lateran Basilica. He was ordained priest on 16 June 1881, in the Church of St Agatha, Rome, at the hands of Mgr Tobias Kirby, Rector of the Irish College and titular Bishop of Litensis. A dispensation of ten months was obtained, because of his age.

Less than a year after arriving in Rome, Marmion found himself once again attracted towards the religious life. The actual moment when he first began to think of becoming a Benedictine monk was while on a visit to Monte Cassino, in September 1880. He later confided to the Prior of Maredsous, D. Robert Cornet: 'It was in Monte Cassino that I first felt the call of God to the monastic life.' However, a more detailed account of this incident is provided by a fellow student, the future Canon Curtain, who had accompanied Marmion to Monte Cassino that day:

> Joseph Marmion and I were good friends. We were in the same class in the College of Propaganda and staying in the

Irish College, Rome. We visited Naples together in September 1880, and were witness to the liquidation of the blood of St Januarius. Returning to Rome, we stopped for a night in Monte Cassino. In the morning Marmion told me that he wanted to remain in Monte Cassino and that he would not return to Rome. There were four of us in the group. I was the eldest and in charge. In fact, we only had permission to go to Naples. Thus, when he told me that he wanted to stay, I told him that he could do nothing of the sort, and I would tell the Abbot (of Monte Cassino) that he had no authorization to do so. Marmion did not insist and returned with us to Rome. He was a holy young man, and full of ideas.

On returning to Rome, Marmion was still filled with the determination to become a Benedictine monk. He decided to talk the matter over with his confessor. The latter told him that everything pointed to his (Marmion) having a religious vocation, and a Benedictine one at that. This led Marmion to give the matter more serious thought. Thus, when his own bishop, Dr McCabe, visited Rome in October 1880, Marmion spoke of the matter to him. Dr McCabe was not opposed to Marmion entering religion, but thought it would be more prudent for Marmion to spend a year or so as a secular priest in Dublin, before making any final decision. He accepted the bishop's terms.

Before coming to a final decision, Marmion sought the advice of his friend, Dr Michael Verdon, the Vice-Rector of the Irish College, Rome. Dr Verdon agreed with Marmion that the best course was for him to return to Ireland, and immediately wrote to Archbishop McCabe on his behalf, explaining the situation:

We have advised him to follow the doctor's orders and return home as soon as possible.

Marmion, when writing to Dr Kirby to thank him for his kindness and attention during the past year-and-a-half, confirmed this reason of health as the main cause of his leaving Rome in the summer of 1881. He also described to Kirby his journey back to Ireland, via Belgium, to visit his friend Joseph Moreau, in the Abbey of Maredsous:

Following the doctor's advice, I delayed on my way home, in order that on my return to Ireland, I might be able to com-

mence work with renewed vigour … A young friend of mine,
who is a novice in the beautiful monastery of Maredsous, invited me to spend a few days with him … I gladly availed
myself of the invitation.

Just as Marmion had been impressed by his visit to Monte
Cassino in September 1880, so now, in August 1881, he was almost swept off his feet by the atmosphere and peace of
Maredsous. His first impressions of the abbey were more than
enthusiastic:

> I arrived at the monastery towards evening, and was im-
> pressed by the peace and silence of the vast cloisters, the
> chant of the divine office, and the feeling of complete separa-
> tion from the world which reigned there.

During his stay in Maredsous, he had a conversation with the
abbot, D. Placide Wolter, and spoke of his intention of becoming
a Benedictine monk (perhaps in New Norcia). He received a
shrewd, and almost prophetic, reply from Abbot Wolter, who
told him: 'You have a much stronger Benedictine vocation than
your friend (Moreau).' It seems certain that these words, spoken
by the Abbot of Maredsous, as well as the general atmosphere of
the monastery, made Marmion think again about his own
monastic leanings. It also set him thinking that his future might
well lie in Maredsous, rather than in New Norcia. However, for
the moment, he had other more pressing matters on his mind.
After remaining only a few days in Maredsous, he continued his
journey back to Ireland. He was not feeling well. Once back in
Ireland he became seriously ill and had to go into hospital. Some
years later, when writing to his friend Dr Patrick Dwyer, he referred to his illness in 1881:

> How is James Murray (Bishop of Maitland)? … I shall never
> forget his kindness in calling to see me when I was sick in
> Dublin after my return from Rome (in August 1881).

We have no details of the medical problem which caused
Marmion to go into hospital. However, it evidently was not too
serious, as he recovered quickly, and was able to take up his new
appointment as curate in the parish of Dundrum, Co Dublin, on
14 September 1881.

Curate in Dundrum, September 1881-September 1882
The appointment of a priest to a curacy, or mission, as it was

often called, was the responsibility of the archbishop and his council. We know that Archbishop McCabe was contemplating taking Marmion as his private secretary. He had written to this effect to Dr Michael Verdon in Rome, in July 1881, asking for a character reference of Marmion, and also asking about the latter's fluency in writing Latin. Dr Verdon had replied to Archbishop McCabe on 24 July 1881:

> I beg to say that in all aspects, Mr Marmion is a very satisfactory student. In character he is thoroughly candid and honest. He writes Latin fluently, but I had never the opportunity of judging his style. Perhaps your Grace might find it convenient to ask him some day to prepare a document for you, and then you could judge for yourself.

Apparently pressure was put on the Archbishop of Dublin to have the young Marmion sent as curate to Dundrum, where the parish priest, Joseph Hickey, was an old friend of the Marmion family. The Hickeys and Marmions were neighbours in Queen Street, Dublin. Fr Hickey had followed with interest the career of Joseph Marmion, both in Clonliffe and Rome, and seems to have taken a fatherly interest in him. Thus, when he learnt of Marmion's return from Rome in August 1881, he immediately approached Archbishop McCabe and asked that Marmion be sent to Dundrum as his curate. He made such a good case that his request was granted, though the archbishop still reserved the right to recall Marmion as his secretary at some future date. Even as late as June 1882, there was question of Marmion leaving Dundrum and being taken into the service of the Archbishop of Dublin:

> For some time past there has been question of appointing me private secretary of his Eminence, Cardinal McCabe. ... (However), my parish priest (Fr Hickey) pressed him not to remove me as yet, and so the matter stands.

In fact, Cardinal McCabe never called Marmion to act as his secretary, but left him in Dundrum, where he immediately threw himself into the busy life of a zealous pastor.

It was a new experience for Marmion. Besides being curate in a large and expanding parish, he held two chaplaincies, one to the sisters of the Sacred Heart Convent, Mount Anville, and the other to the large Mental Asylum in Dundrum. He had to rise at

5.45 am and say Mass at 7.10. Then he did his round of chronic sick-calls, and so the day was passed, visiting schools, preaching, meeting members of the St Vincent de Paul Society, etc., not to mention hearing confessions, and participating at baptisms, weddings and funerals. The confessional took up a lot of his time, and he seems to have found this part of his ministry very congenial and satisfying. In fact, he confided in a friend that he 'preferred the hearing of confessions to any other duty.' He told this same correspondent, Fr Dwyer, in February 1882: 'I haven't much time to be idle.' He was daily brought into contact with a cross-section of humanity, and called upon to advise, teach, console and give every kind of spiritual and material aid.

It was not that he courted popularity, but he obviously had a way with people, as one of his parishioners, who knew him in Dundrum, later testified:

> Fr Joseph Marmion was a grand young man, very popular and welcome in every family. Full of life and jolly. Very good with children especially.

Another witness, Mr Shield, the clerk or sacristan in Dundrum church at this time, wrote that Marmion was 'so gentle and good, but very delicate'.

Marmion possessed an extraordinary facility for adapting himself to other people. Above all, he excelled in comforting others and putting them at their ease. There is a story told of him during his time in Dundrum, that he went to say Mass in a small church for the first time. The sacristan was his aunt, a rather scrupulous lady by nature. When she saw him coming, she became so excited that she seized the hands of the young priest in her own, expressing her great happiness. However, during the Mass she suffered terrible scruples, imagining that her conduct had distracted her nephew from preparing properly for Mass. After the Mass, she asked forgiveness, with tears in her eyes. The next day, when he came to say Mass, she was looking very serious, with her eyes lowered to the ground. Marmion, seeing her thus and knowing her feelings, immediately took her in his arms and began to dance with her around the sacristy.

However, it was above all in his dealings with the sick, the poor and the elderly, that Marmion built up a reputation for holiness during his time as curate in Dundrum. His sister Rosie (Mother

Peter) recounted one incident, when, having nothing else to give a poor woman, he gave her his watch, which was of considerable value. Such examples of practical charity could be multiplied. The plain fact is, that Joseph Marmion built up such a reputation for charity and sanctity, that his memory, even a hundred years later, is still held in high regard in Dundrum today. Proof of this is the existence of the Dom Marmion Society, founded in Dundrum by Fr Stephen Greene in 1969, to perpetuate the memory of the former curate. The aim of the Marmion Society is 'to ease the plight of the lonely, the aged, the sick and handicapped of Dundrum village.' Also in the village is a community hall, called the Dom Marmion House, where elderly people can meet and have a chat over light refreshments. Recently (1992), a new and enlarged Dom Marmion House was built, on a more accessible site, and constitutes an impressive monument to the young priest who worked in the parish for only one year. Membership of the Dom Marmion Society is drawn from people in all walks of life, who are committed to helping others less fortunate than themselves.

Obviously he was kept so busy as a curate in Dundrum that he had little or no time to undertake the necessary correspondence connected with making any formal application to join a monastery. He had also promised his archbishop that he would remain for some time working in Dublin, to repay his debt to the diocese. He was still very young, only twenty-three years of age, and as head of the family, had certain responsibilities towards his mother and brother. At the same time, it is evident that the idea of becoming a Benedictine monk never left his mind completely, and he only awaited a suitable opportunity to fulfil this desire.

A personal problem which he had to face during this time in Dundrum was his health. He speaks in several of his letters, of an attack of some recurring illness. Thus he told Fr Dwyer, in February 1882: 'Ever since my last letter, I had a partial attack, but now it is wholly and finally removed, together with its effect and cause.' One of the results of his stay in Rome was a recurring bout of malaria. He had a serious attack on his return to Ireland in August 1881, and another in November of that same year. During this second illness, he was looked after by the sisters of the Convent of the Sacred Heart, where he served as chaplain. The Reverend Mother was very concerned about him, and sent him 'a dozen of rare Spanish wine' and also on occasion sent around her carriage to collect him in the morning. Sometimes he was too ill to say Mass, as the sister sacristan recalled at the time:

> Father Marmion was always such an example to us all. He suffered from malaria, and often after a night of fever, when he had to break his fast, he dragged himself to the Convent Chapel to give us Holy Communion, lest we be disappointed.

He had his third and, thankfully, last attack of malaria in January 1882. All this must have been a great worry to the young curate. In addition to the attacks of malaria, he also had some problem with his back, which led to partial paralysis of the spine. In the light of such health problems, he had to be practical when considering his future situation. Living alone as a curate in Dundrum was not ideal, and evidently the thought of living in community, which would be his lot if he became a professor at Clonliffe, had its attractions. From every point of view, therefore, it seemed prudent for him to take up the post offered him by his archbishop. He resigned his curacy in Dundrum in mid-September 1882, leaving behind many friends, and a reputation which was to outlive him.

Professor at Clonliffe, September 1882-October 1886

It was, in many ways, providential that Marmion now took up the professorship in Clonliffe. While not underestimating the excellent work he had done as curate in Dundrum, and the value of this experience, it must be said that the pastoral ministry had its limitation. Above all, during his time in Dundrum, he had been unable to pursue his studies. The study of sacred scripture and the reading of the spiritual classics is an essential part of a priest's life. It is an on-going thing, but it requires time and a peaceful atmosphere. There was the danger that Marmion might have lost the taste for study, had he remained longer on the mission. Given his calling to the religious and monastic life and above all, his future responsibilities as Retreat Master, Prior of Louvain and Abbot of Maredsous, these four years as professor in Clonliffe helped to complete his intellectual and spiritual formation. Thrown into the atmosphere of college life, he soon found himself in his native element.

During these four years in Clonliffe, one of his greatest joys was his work as chaplain to the Redemptoristine sisters in Drumcondra. He said Mass there every morning, and became close friends with many of the community. The Redemptoristines had come to Dublin from Belgium in 1859. Their foundress was Mother John of the Cross (Julie Verheest, 1826-1902) who remained superior of the convent from 1859-91. She immediately struck up a rapport with this fervent young priest, and was later to encourage him in his Benedictine vocation.

The Annals of the Convent show that he was appointed chaplain on 1 September 1882, and that he held this position until October 1886. There are numerous references to Marmion in the Annals. However, the most moving experience of his chaplaincy days with the Redemptoristines came in August 1884, when he was asked to assist at the death of one of the novices, Sister M. Clare, only a month before her profession. He was given special permission to attend the dying sister, to give her Viaticum, and receive her vows. He spent several nights up with her, praying all the time and helping her support the pain. Marmion described the experience in a letter to a nun friend. It was the first of many such scenes which he witnessed throughout his priestly life:

> One of the novices, who was about a month from her profession, was taken ill last week; although the malady appeared insignificant, she knew from the beginning that she would never recover. I was delighted to hear her confession, assist her in her agony, and if necessary to receive her religious profession. At about 3.30 on Monday morning I was called, as she had become much worse. It happened most providently that just at that time she had a good interval, so I was able to give her Holy Viaticum, and she made her holy profession, received the black veil and ring. I prayed quietly with her and stood by her all the time. A few moments before death, complete peace returned, and with great happiness, calmly, as though going to sleep she breathed forth her soul.

During the last days of Sister Clare's life, Marmion confided to her an anxious doubt that troubled him, regarding some part of the ceremony of his ordination to the priesthood. He asked Sister Clare to speak of it to Mary and St Joseph, whom she would meet soon. In fact, he received an answer the same night on which she died, when Sister Clare appeared to him saying that all was right. From that moment, he was at peace, and never again worried about the matter.

Apart from his contact with the Redemptoristines in Dublin, Marmion kept in touch with his three sisters who were nuns. One of these, Sister Columba, had recently been appointed superior of a new foundation of the Sisters of Mercy at Dunmore East, Co Waterford. They were in need of novices, and Marmion sent a young Dublin girl to them in 1885, to join the community. He wrote several times to this novice, giving her advice and encouragement. He availed of this letter-writing to examine his own conscience, and reflect on his own possible religious vocation. Thus he wrote to this Dunmore East novice on 27 November 1885:

> If I were joining religion tomorrow, I would enter with the determination of leaving myself absolutely in the hands of my superiors, to let them cut away mercilessly all the excrescences of my character, so that I might be fit to be presented, as a clean oblation, on the altar of God's love.

In August 1885, Marmion paid his second visit to Maredsous, with his fellow professor at Clonliffe, Rev John Healy. The latter gave the following account of this visit:

> Joe (Joseph) Marmion did nothing but speak of Maredsous, and in the end convinced me to go with him to Maredsous for a visit. After many adventures, we arrived there, and even I was enchanted with the visit.

It was during this second visit to Maredsous, that Marmion finally decided to become a monk in that particular abbey, believing that by entering there he would find a surer path to perfection.

On his return to Dublin in September 1885, Marmion went to see the newly-appointed Archbishop of Dublin, Dr William Walsh. He made a formal request to be allowed to resign his professorship in Clonliffe, and join the Benedictine Abbey of Maredsous in Belgium.

On 25 October 1886, the Archbishop of Dublin, Dr Walsh, gave Marmion his Dimissorial Letters, granting him permission to join the Benedictine Order. A few days later, Marmion wrote to the Abbot of Maredsous, D. Placide Wolter, announcing his arrival in Belgium, to join the Maredsous community in mid-November.

When the actual moment came to leave Ireland, Marmion told only a few close friends and relations the day and the hour. Those who actually knew of his departure from Ireland were: his mother, his sister Rosie (M. Peter), his bishop (Dr Walsh), his director of conscience (Fr Gowan), the president of Clonliffe (Dr Fitzpatrick), and one of his students, Frank Wall, with whom he passed part of his last night in Dublin. While many of his acquaintances knew about his desire to enter religion, they had no idea where he was going, or when. Thus, to these latter, his departure seemed sudden, and they were somewhat taken aback. He was accused of being unpatriotic in leaving his country, just when men of his calibre were needed. Some priest friends, in Ireland and Rome, roundly abused him for being a kind of apostate, in leaving the diocesan clergy. From his own point of view, the decision to leave Clonliffe was not a turning of his back on anyone or anything, so much as a turning of his face towards a path marked out for him by God. It was not a betrayal, but rather the taking up of a challenge. Some people predicted that he would not persevere in his monastic vocation, and that very soon he would be back again in Dublin. Even his most intimate friends were sceptical, and one of them, Frank Wall, later wrote that he had even said as much to Marmion on the eve of his departure for Maredsous.

However, Marmion was not to be deterred, and on a mid-November morning, accompanied by his friend, Fr Bartholomew Fitzpatrick, he left Clonliffe to catch the boat-train, which would take him on the first leg of his journey to Maredsous. His heart was filled with joy, for he had confidence that God would sustain him in the days ahead. At the same time, he knew he left many sad hearts behind him. It had not been easy for him to leave his widowed mother and his two younger brothers. He later reflected on this human side of a religious vocation, and said: 'Ordinarily, on entering religion, one's greatest pain is the pain we cause others.' He was speaking of his own experience on that morning he left Dublin, to become a monk in Maredsous, Belgium.

CHAPTER 3

The Young Monk
(1886-1899)

The Novice, November 1886-February 1888

As the young ex-curate, ex-professor from Ireland approached the gates of Maredsous on 21 November 1886, he made a symbolic gesture of self-denial, by throwing out of the window of the carriage a silver tobacco box, which he had brought in his pocket. Evidently he had smoked from time to time during his days in Dublin. As far as we know, he never smoked again. In any case, he was determined to be the perfect novice, ready for everything. If asked what were his principal motives in joining Maredsous, he would have answered: 'To do the will of God, and to obey.' Marmion was, of course, no novice to the spiritual life. He had already developed within himself a life of prayer, and he had his priesthood. These two things would sustain him through the trials and vicissitudes of the novitiate in Maredsous.

Yet despite his age (27), and his maturity of mind and soul, there is no doubt that Marmion's entrance to the Benedictine monastery of Maredsous was a traumatic experience. His monastic vocation implied deep down in his soul a real conversion. It is evident from everything that he did and said during his first weeks in Maredsous, that he was going through the same kind of spiritual struggle as a would-be convert to catholicism. It was a genuine break with the past, a new beginning, an act of faith in the power of God's grace to transform him from a diocesan priest into a Benedictine monk. He was clothed as a postulant on 24 November 1886, and the first entry in his private notes dated 30 November 1886, sums up his initial feelings of shock:

> I had the impression on the day of entering Maredsous, that in entering the monastery, I had just done the most senseless thing in the world.

However, these gloomy thoughts were not to last, and very soon
he had settled down to the routine life of a trainee-monk. The
first letter we have from these days was written on 3 January
1887, to three fellow-monks of Maredsous, who had been sent to
study philosophy in Seckau, Austria. It is full of the camaraderie
and good humour which Marmion always showed in such circumstances.

> Here I am beginning my first letter in French! Not an easy
> thing, but when one is writing to one's brethren, difficulties
> do not count ... We are a very happy family here in the novi-
> tiate, and it bears out the fact that variety is the spice of life.
> There is the tall Benedict and the small Germain; then
> Brother Schyrgens who is a great talker, and Brother Roisin
> who is always laughing, and finally, of course, this Irish man,
> who doesn't understand anything that is going on, and
> Brother Hilary who is a saint!

Throughout the time of his novitiate, Marmion was under the
authority of the novice-master, D. Benoît D'Hondt. All are
agreed that he was a hard task-master, very austere and mortified. Yet he held this office from 1882 to 1905. His one great dic-
tum was that 'the monk should obey and submit humbly and
even joyfully to his superior'. There are numerous stories of his
obsession with mortifying the novices. One of Marmion's contemporaries was an artist who had moved his standing-desk
near the window, in order to admire the view. The novice-master came into his cell, and noticed how the furniture had been
changed about. He asked the reason, and on being told, immediately ordered the novice, not only to take the standing-desk
away from the window, but forbade the novice ever to look out
of the window again. The novices had absolutely no privacy.
They never knew when the novice-master would come into their
room, or worse still, when he would look through the spy-hole
which was affixed to the centre of each cell, as in a prison. Some
of the stories told would suggest that D. Benoît D'Hondt was a
sadist; but more likely, there was a strong element of Jansenism
in his spirituality. He evidently lacked both common sense and
prudence, especially in regard to the health of his novices,
whom he mortified in every way possible, depriving them of
any normal comfort and relaxation. There was no central heating in the monastery at this time, and fires were not allowed in
the individual cells. While there is no evidence that the notiviate

regime in Maredsous undermined Marmion's health, it must have been in stark contrast to his life as a professor in Clonliffe.

As a novice, Marmion was very restricted in the number of letters he could write. This fact hurt him deeply, as he felt he was letting down those who were nearest and dearest to him, especially when he could not reply to the letters he received. One day, soon after entering Maredsous, his innermost self crushed to its very fibre, with tears in his eyes, he went to throw himself before the tabernacle, and said to Our Lord:

> And yet, my Jesus, I know you want me to be here. And so I would rather let myself be cut to pieces than leave the monastery.

This cry of anguish was probably caused by his frustration, in not being able to reply to all those who had written to him during these first few months in Maredsous. In one of the few surviving letters, dated June 1887, written to his close friend, Mother Gabriel, OP, he refers to his 'uncourteous silence with which I have treated your letter,' and explains his predicament:

> I am but a poor little novice, and though on receiving each kind letter, I was dying to write to you, I could never manage it. The thought that my dear friends in Beaumont would think that I have forgotten them, often constituted a very heavy interior mortification for me.

He had the same problem in corresponding with his best friend, Rev P.V. Dwyer, who was in Australia. When eventually, after completing his novitiate, he was allowed to write to Australia, he told Fr Dwyer that 'our faculties for letter-writing, usually limited, are almost suspended during the novitiate.

Towards the end of his notiviate, Marmion suffered a great personal loss in the sudden death of his fellow priest-novice, Rev Br Athanase Roisin. The latter was Marmion's junior in age by one year, and was a most lovable character. He had been Professor of French, Drawing and Music in an Industrial School in Tournai, before entering Maredsous on 22 October 1886, one month before Marmion's own entry. Both novices had a great deal in common besides their priesthood, and provided each other with mutual support. Br Athanase was due for simple profession on 6 January 1888, but quite unexpectedly, two days before this, on 4 January, he was struck down with what was diagnosed as a brain tumour. Death came very suddenly, and there was no time to have him pronounce his vows.

When the community of Maredsous met in Chapter on 19 January 1888, to discuss Marmion's suitability for simple profession, he was admitted by unanimous vote. This fact alone would indicate that there was no question-mark over his character or conduct during this time of probation as a novice. A few days before his simple profession, he had a pleasant surprise, when Mgr Donnelly, the Auxiliary Bishop of Dublin, came to visit him, and stayed for the profession ceremony. It was a welcome link with his family and friends in Dublin. The Annals of Maredsous give a short account of the profession:

> On 10 February, 1888, the Feast of St Scholastica, Br Remacle Schyrgens, of Liège, and Br Columba Marmion, of the diocese of Dublin (formerly a pupil at the College of Propaganda, Rome), made their simple Profession.

There is a ring of truth in the story that when, on the eve of his profession, his novice-master asked him what had been his greatest trial during his novitiate, Marmion replied quite simply: 'You yourself!' There were certainly no hard feelings, and we known that D. Benoît D'Hondt, the novice-master, held Marmion in such high regard that sometime in 1889 he had him appointed as his assistant novice-master.

The Simply Professed Monk, 10 February 1888-10 February 1891
10 February 1888 marked not only the day of Marmion's simple profession, but also the end of his novitiate. The fact that he was already a priest, meant that he did not have to undergo the usual course of studies in philosophy and theology. He was, therefore, free to take up whatever job or position his abbot, (D. Placide Wolter) assigned to him. His first job was teaching in the abbey school, while also acting as a kind of house-master to the junior boys. The position did not suit him, as his French was still rather poor and he had never been trained to look after very young people. It is not surprising that he failed lamentably, and he was asked instead to teach philosophy to the junior monks. This was more congenial and more in his line, as Abbot Placide Wolter confirmed:

> Our Fr Columba is hebdomadary this week. He is managing very well. In general he is doing very well. I have noticed

how well he understood the philosophy of St Thomas. I now understand the excellent references he was given on coming here.

As time went on, Marmion became more and more convinced that he had found his true vocation in Maredsous. As he confided to his friend Fr Dwyer, 'I am convinced that I am where God wills me to be. I have found great peace, and am extremely happy.' Undoubtedly there were high and low moments in his life. One of the high moments must have been 19 August 1888, when the abbey church of Maredsous was dedicated. It was a most splendid occasion, attended by the Papal Nuncio, Cardinal Schiaffino, along with several Belgian bishops, and a large number of Benedictine abbots, not to mention the two founding Desclée brothers, Henri and Jules. One could say that Maredsous came of age that August day 1888. In one sense, Maredsous acted as a symbol, as well as a model, of the reflowering and resurgence of the Benedictine Order, not only in Belgium, but all over the world, in the second half of the nineteenth century. Marmion felt he was part of this monastic renaissance, and wanted to make his own contribution to it. For a Benedictine monk, attachment to the monastery of his profession is a virtue and comes under his vow of Stability. He sinks his roots in one place, and would normally expect to spend the rest of his life in that one monastery. One can understand, therefore, why Marmion was determined to persevere. Maredsous had become not only part of his life, but the centre of his life. A good pen-picture of Maredsous at this time, is given by a future novice, Henry (John) Chapman:

> Maredsous is a wonderful little bit of the Middle Ages. A huge, great monastery of blue stone, built on top of a hill, round three sides of a cloister, the fourth side being the church, as large as a cathedral (and wider than English cathedrals). The whole completed only a very few years ago, by the generosity of two Belgians, brothers. The monks are most charming, cheerful and timid, and very holy, it does one good to look at them.

During the summer of 1890, the Abbey of Maredsous found itself facing the election of a new abbot. This was occasioned by the election of D. Placide Wolter, the first Abbot of Maredsous, as Archabbot of Beuron, in succession to his brother, D. Maur

Wolter, who had died on 4 July 1890. The monks of Maredsous elected D. Hildebrand de Hemptinne, a Belgian, as the second Abbot of Maredsous on 10 August. He remained Abbot of Maredsous from 1890 to 1909. An outstanding man in every sense of the word, he was destined in three years time to become the first Abbot Primate of the Benedictine Order.

Marmion made his solemn profession in the abbey church of Maredsous on 10 February 1891. By then, he had been nearly five years in the monastery, and had undergone a very thorough initiation into the Benedictine way of life. He was beginning to speak French with ease, and would soon be able to hear confessions and preach in that language.

The Professed Monk, 1891-1899
Within a week of his solemn profession, Marmion found himself something of a local celebrity. The parish priest of Graux, a small town about three miles from Maredsous, came to ask for one of the monks to preach in his church on 16 February 1891. The Prior of Maredsous (D. Robert de Kerchove) told him that he had no one he could send. Then on second thoughts he said: 'There is a young foreign monk, but I don't think I can send him, as his French is still imperfect, so I doubt if he would be of any use to you.' 'Let me have him all the same,' said the priest, 'It will be a change for my parishioners anyway.' Three days later, the parish priest brought Marmion back, and declared that never before had he experienced such a preacher in his parish. The young Irish monk had made a great impression on the people. From that time onward, the 'Irish Father' was in constant demand in the region.

Towards the end of 1894 and the beginning of 1895, Marmion suffered a set-back in regard to his health. He wrote in his private notes, under 17 February 1895:

> I have been ill for several months, and besides some physical suffering, e.g. sleeplessness etc. I was greatly troubled in mind, and seemed at time quite abandoned by God. On the feast of St Scholastica, the anniversary of my profession, the clouds passed away.

It was quite clear that Marmion needed some kind of holiday or change of air. His superiors must have noticed his condition, because in mid-1895, they offered him a trip to Ireland. It was nine years since he had left Ireland, and the thought of re-visiting his native country and seeing his old friends must have come as a welcome surprise. The first mention we have of this visit is in a letter to Mlle de Brouwer, written on Good Friday 1895:

> Pray for me. There is the possibility of visiting my own country. Ask Our Lord to arrange everything for His glory, as I desire nothing which does not please him.

He and another monk of Maredsous, D. Grégoire Fournier, were sent to represent Abbot Hildebrand de Hemptinne, at the centenary celebrations of St Patrick's College, Maynooth. At this time, Abbot Hildebrand was not only Abbot of Maredsous, but also Abbot Primate. We possess a detailed account of their journey and stay in Ireland. They set out on 10 June 1895, dressed in the style of clergymen, with Roman collar, suit, and even overcoat and hat. They travelled by boat, via Ostende, London, Bristol and Queenstown (Cobh). Their first visit on landing in Ireland, was to Clonakilty, Co Cork, to the Convent of Mercy, where they had the pleasure of meeting Marmion's sister, M. Peter (Rosie). They then went to Dunmore East, Co Waterford, where another sister, M. Columba, was superior. D. Grégoire remarked the great likeness, in both physique and character, that existed between Marmion and this sister. The two monks then proceeded to Dublin, where they were entertained by Marmion's married sister, Mrs Joyce, and her family. However, there was one sad note in this visit to his native Dublin, in that his mother, Mrs Marmion, was not there to greet him. Thus he had no real home, and he and D. Grégoire stayed in a small hotel.

Wednesday 26 June was the big day in Maynooth, and the two monks, dressed this time in their Benedictine habits, made their way by train to Maynooth. They arrived just in time for the pontifical Mass, said by Archbishop Walsh of Dublin. They took their places in the body of the church, with hundreds of other priests, sisters and lay people. After Mass there was lunch for everyone in a large marquee. So far, the two monks from Maredsous had met no one in authority, or been introduced to any of the dignitaries who had gathered for the centenary. They met several priests who recognised Marmion and called him 'Father Joe', but otherwise they were entirely incognito. The lunch was followed by a lengthy academic *séance*, which included numerous speeches. However, the highlight of the day's celebrations was to be the banquet. Just before this event, Marmion and D. Grégoire met the President of Maynooth College (Mgr Gargan), who greeted them cordially, but showed some surprise that they had not made themselves known earlier. It was all very embarrassing, as the two monks had no idea they were to be accorded such honour. Thus for the rest of the evening they had to mix with the higher dignitaries. Among these latter was a certain Mgr Mercier, the future Cardinal of Malines, Belgium. Marmion and Mercier met for the first time in Maynooth, and immediately struck up a friendship which lasted all their lives.

Marmion and D. Grégoire spent their final days in Dungannon, where Marmion's brother, Matthew, lived. Altogether, the trip had been a nostalgic and moving experience for both the monks. Neither had solicited the privilege of representing the Abbot Primate and Maredsous at the Maynooth celebrations. Evidently, they were impressed by the honour done them, and Abbot Primate Hildebrand, on that occasion. Marmion returned to Maredsous refreshed, and thankful to God and his abbot for these few weeks in Ireland.

On his return to Maredsous, Marmion once again took up his round of monastic duties: assistant Novice-Master, assistant Master of Ceremonies, and Professor of Philosophy to the monks in simple vows. On top of all this, he was soon very much involved in giving conferences and retreats to different groups, both inside and outside the monastery. He found a special apostolate among the clergy of the dioceses of Namur and Liège. This latter apostolate began with an invitation to give a monthly day of recollection to priests gathered in Dinant, and thus began an association with this group which lasted two years. He worked very hard to develop a style of speaking which would be both attractive and helpful to his audience.

There was talk in 1896 of his being sent to Brazil, and he was quite happy to go, if ordered to do so. There was also much talk in Maredsous, during the closing years of the 1890s, of a new foundation in Louvain. By 1897, he had been relieved of his duties as assistant novice-master, perhaps to allow him more time for retreats and conferences. He jokingly told his friend Fr Dwyer that the real reason was his inability, when out walking, to keep up with the number of young postulants, as he had become 'almost as stout as Dom Feuillen'.

CHAPTER 4

Louvain

(1899-1909)

The Foundation of Mont César

In April 1888, the Abbot of Maredsous (D. Placide Wolter) sent one of his monks, D. Gérard van Caloen, to Louvain to open a 'House of Studies' there for the past pupils of Maredsous Abbey School. At the same time, D. Gérard van Caloen was on the look-out for a suitable site on which to establish a Benedictine monastery. He eventually decided in early 1889, on a property called 'Mont César' or 'Kaiserberg,' overlooking the university city. In March 1889, D. Robert de Kerchove, at the time Prior of Maredsous, was sent to Louvain, to replace D. Gérard van Caloen, who was destined for the mission in Brazil. D. Robert was given a double mandate:

1. To establish a University Hostel and
2. To set in motion all the necessary preparations for a monastic foundation in Louvain, where the young monks of Maredsous could study theology in a university setting.

D. Robert de Kerchove was a man of very considerable administration ability, as well as possessing great energy. He decided to buy the property called 'Mont César'. It proved to be a long and expensive process, which lasted six years (1889-1895).

In September 1894, Abbot Hildebrand obtained permission from Cardinal Goossens, the Archbishop of Malines, to found a Benedictine monastery in Louvain. This cleared the last hurdle in the way of the Maredsous monks. In April 1896, the final plans for the monastery were drawn up by Abbot Hildebrand, in association with a Louvain architect, Mr Langerock, but the actual building was delayed until March 1897. It was proposed to call the abbey 'Regina Coeli' (Queen of Heaven).

By the beginning of 1899, one wing of the monastery had been built, and 13 April 1899 was fixed as the day when the founding

monks would leave Maredsous for Louvain. D. Robert de
Kerchove was appointed prior of the new monastery, and
Marmion was to be subprior and prefect of clerics. At the same
time Marmion was to be spiritual director of the Carmelite
Sisters of Louvain. A few days before leaving for Louvain,
Marmion had written to the Mother Prioress of the Carmelite
Convent saying:

> The little band (14 in all) of the sons of St Benedict will enter
> Louvain Thursday next, the Feast of St Ida. I am writing to
> ask your prayers, and those of your children, during these
> days, in order that the demon, who will most certainly be
> angry at our arrival, may not make any difficulties, and that
> the good God may bless us.

It seems that the monks of Maredsous had expected some hostil-
ity from the people of Louvain, especially from those who had
lived in or around 'Mont César'. Many of these had to be re-
housed elsewhere to make room for the monastery. Marmion referred to this in a letter he wrote to Abbot Hildebrand on 15
April 1899:

> Up to this, God has blessed us in every way. It seems as if our
> dear Mother Mary had taken matters into her own hands ...
> Far from having encountered any mark of hostility, we met
> with many remarks of respect, and the Cross was frequently
> saluted by those we met.

However, it would be wrong to think that everything was a bed
of roses for the Irish monk, now transplanted from Maredsous
to Louvain. Evidence given during the Namur Diocesan Enquiry,
by two witnesses, suggests that the Irish monk found it very
painful to leave Maredsous for Louvain. He is recorded as having said that 'it was one of the greatest trials of my life'. According
to another witness:

> He (Marmion) left Maredsous with certain misgivings. He
> knew D. Robert de Kerchove and was well aware of the dif-
> ferences between their two characters. But he abandoned
> himself to the will of God.

This difference of character was to cause much suffering to
Marmion during his time in Louvain and became almost a daily
cross. His native exuberance and love of fun contrasted with the
cold and serious outlook of D. Robert. A further difference lay in

the fact that D. Robert wished his monks to stay within the cloister all the time, whereas Marmion was full of 'apostolic zeal and
inclined to respond to appeals which came to him from outside
the monastery.' However, this incompatibility did not lead to
any serious quarrel or clash between the two. Marmion was
always ready to submit to his superior, a fact he made quite
evident, when D. Robert was appointed the first Abbot of Mont
César in September 1899, and Marmion appointed prior of the
monastery. Marmion underpinned this element of obedience, in
the address which he made to Abbot Robert de Kerchove, on behalf of the community, when the abbot returned to Louvain after
his abbatial blessing in Maredsous. A further proof that both
abbot and prior had an excellent working relationship, was the
fact that Marmion was re-appointed prior each of the ten years
he spent in Louvain.

Early days in Louvain

One considerable difference between Louvain and Maredsous
was the question of language. Louvain lay in the Flemish-speak-
ing part of Belgium, whereas Maredsous was in the French-
speaking (Walloon) region. Thus Marmion, who had only recently succeeded in mastering the French language, now found
himself having to speak Flemish. He elaborated on this matter in
a letter to D. Bede Camm, in May 1899:

> Talking of languages, I am pounding the Flemish, as it is nec-
> essary here. One of my penitents at the Carmelite Convent
> speaks only Flemish, and as I think it is highly probable now
> that I am destined to live and die in this dear country of my
> adoption, I must know its tongue.

In many ways, the life which Marmion was now experiencing
reminded him of his time as professor in Clonliffe, Dublin. He
was once again in a university milieu, teaching theology and
giving spiritual conferences and retreats. He wrote at length to
his friend, Bishop P. V. Dwyer in Australia:

> This kind of life of study, teaching and contact with the uni-
> versity, is according to my natural tastes; but as I have not
> chosen it, I am sure it is God's will for the present; and I suc-
> ceed very well in it.

Marmion exercised an extraordinary influence over the minds
and souls of the young monks committed to his care. Most of
them had been subjected to a very narrow initiation into monas-

tic life by D. Benoît D'Hondt, the novice-master in Maredsous for more then twenty years (1883-1905). Marmion had to counter-act this rather Jansenistic spirituality, and became the spiritual Father to a whole generation of monks. As prefect of clerics, he gave two conferences a week on monastic spirituality, including the main themes of the Rule of St Benedict: discretion, obedi-ence, love of Christ and so on. But it was above all by his exam-ple of piety and his constant good humour, that he encouraged the younger monks to a life of prayer and union with God. There was general agreement among those who attended his lectures and conferences, that 'he lived what he preached'.

The pastoral care of the dying

Before coming to Louvain, Marmion had been much involved in the pastoral care of the sick and the dying, in the neighbourhood around Maredsous. One particular family, the Bodarts, had come to depend very much on him. His relationship with this family shows, not only his love of God and zeal for souls, but also how he was able to mix the human and the supernatural into a happy blend. In 1897, Madame Bodart was struck down with an incurable disease which, thanks to the care of Marmion, she gradually came to accept. He assured her that God would watch over her husband and four young children after her death, and that he (Marmion) would be with her during her last hours on this earth. However, she had not died by the time he left for Louvain, and his departure left an emptiness and an utter desolation in the Bodart family, which increased as Madame Bodart became weaker and weaker.

Eventually, in February 1900, Monsieur Bodart wired to Mont César to tell Marmion that the end was near, begging him to come immediately. However, Abbot Robert refused to give Marmion the necessary permission to make the journey, main-taining that his presence was not really needed by the Bodarts. Marmion was greatly distressed at this turn of events, not be-cause of his own feelings, but because Madame Bodart had ex-pressed a wish to see him before she died, and she would think that he had abandoned her. He immediately went to throw him-self in front of the Blessed Sacrament, and said to Our Lord:

> You Lord, have confided to me this soul; I have given you my liberty; but these two things no longer work together. Please arrange it otherwise.

He left the church, convinced that everything would work out all right. However, during the night the idea of leaving Louvain pressed hard upon his mind but he rejected it as a temptation, realising that for him the most important thing was obedience to his abbot. The following morning a letter came to Abbot Robert from a parish priest who lived near Namur, asking him to send Marmion immediately to preach a three-day retreat. Abbot Robert called his prior and ordered him to go to preach the retreat in Namur. Just before leaving the abbot asked Marmion if the Bodarts lived near the parish he was about to visit. On being told 'Yes,' the abbot lifted his original ban and told Marmion that he could call to see Madame Bodart. Thus it was that Marmion arrived in time to hear her confession and give her the last rites of the Church. He always believed that God had rewarded his act of obedience, and saw the whole affair as 'providential'.

Tests of obedience
Among his many duties during these years in Louvain, Marmion was 'extraordinary' confessor to the nuns of St Scholastica at Maredret. This assignment involved visiting Maredret four times a year, to give a spiritual conference and hear the confessions of the community. Already, before leaving Maredsous for Louvain in 1899, Marmion had frequently visited Maredret and formed a close spiritual friendship with several of the sisters. From Louvain, Marmion kept in touch with his spiritual daughters in Maredret, mainly by letter. For some reason or other, in 1902, the correspondence between Marmion and the Abbess of Maredret increased considerably. This fact did not escape the notice of Abbot Robert. At this time, in most religious houses, all incoming letters were opened by the superior, though not necessarily read, while all outgoing letters were likewise left open, to be closed by the superior.

Quite unexpectedly, Abbot Robert decided to censor the letters passing between his prior and the Abbess of Maredret. Sometime towards the end of March 1902, Marmion was called to his abbot's room, and told that, in future, all the letters passing between Marmion and D. Cécile would be read by him (Abbot Robert). It was an extraordinary thing to do, and the only explanation seems to have been an urge on the part of Abbot Robert 'to exercise an act of authority'. This action by his abbot provided Marmion with a dilemma, as it seemed to imply one of two things: (i) that the abbot suspected something dishonourable was going on between his prior and the Abbess of Maredret, or (ii) that the abbot wished to restrict or reduce his prior's direction of souls.

Marmion immediately decided that he should notify D. Cécile of Abbot Robert's decision, and wrote to her to this effect at the end of March 1902. Apparently his letter never reached her. Marmion, therefore, had to write a second letter, dated 1 April 1902, in which he said:

> I sent you, Saturday (28 March) a little word, explaining that Father Abbot informs me he intends exercising his right to read our letters. You do not seem to have received my letter.

What was he to do? He was quite justified in informing D. Cécile that her letters would be read by Abbot Robert. On the other hand, there was no question of going behind the back of his abbot, and posting his letters down town in Louvain. In any case, all in-coming letters would still be opened. He had no other option but to submit, humbly and with faith, to the action taken by his abbot. He explained his situation in a letter to D. Cécile:

> You will be happy to know that the Lord has given me a great grace, I would say the greatest grace in all my life. For in spite of a terrible internal struggle, He has given me the grace, not only to submit without any reserve to my abbot, but also to retain for him all my confidence and affection.

The decision of Abbot Robert to control or censor his spiritual correspondence hit Marmion in a very vulnerable spot. As a spiritual director, he received many confidences, even secrets. He believed that his correspondents wrote to him as if they were in confession and, as a priest, he had a great respect for the 'seal of the confessional'. He did not want any other eyes to read what was intended for his eyes only. This was one reason why he did not keep the letters of conscience which his penitents wrote to him. Yet, here was his superior, to whom he owed complete obedience, infringing not so much his privacy, but the sacred privacy of his penitents. Given all the circumstances, the decision taken by Marmion to accept the action of his abbot, called for an act of obedience which was certainly supernatural, if not heroic. It was not an easy decision to take yet it was one which he never regretted. Some time later that year (1902), he wrote a long letter to Abbot Hildebrand de Hemptinne, in which he summed up his thoughts on the question of 'perfect submission to superiors.'

This particular trial lasted four months, after which time Abbot Robert lifted the censorship. Many years later, in 1942, Abbot Robert, reflecting on this incident, told P. Raymond Thibaut:

> I have never met a more obedient religious ... I had to make him suffer. It was necessary in order to keep him in the abbey, since he was being sought from all sides to give retreats. But he was Prior, Prefect of Clerics and Professor. I could not give in.

It is quite evident that Abbot Robert continued to admire and value the work and service of Marmion, whom he retained as his prior for ten consecutive years (1900-1909).

For his part, Marmion felt no resentment towards his abbot. He continued to correspond with D. Cécile de Hemptinne and M. Marie-Joseph van Arden, though henceforth he wrote the word 'conscience' on the top of each letter. His final reflections of this affair were contained in a letter to D. Cécile, dated 10 August 1902, assuring her that:

> When one gives oneself absolutely to Our Lord, one does Him great wrong in worrying over little things. Now that the sacrifice has been made, Our Lord has given back to me, by the path of obedience, everything that I had abandoned to him.

Retreat-Master par excellence

Marmion had a special talent or charism for giving retreats. It was during his time in Louvain that he built up a reputation as someone who could hold his audience's interest, and get across the message of the gospel in simple but direct language. D. John Champan wrote that 'no one gives such retreats.' We have numerous accounts of people who admitted that a retreat given by Marmion had been a landmark in their lives. He realised that people thirsted for knowledge and conviction about the truths of the Christian faith.

He was only a few months in Louvain when he was asked to give the annual retreat to the Benedictine monks of Erdington Abbey, Birmingham. The following year, 1900, he preached the annual retreat to the monks of Maredsous and also to his own community at Mont César. Abbot Robert, writing to D. Cécile de Hemptinne on 30 October 1900, said:

> Our Retreat ended this morning. Everyone was very satisfied with it. It was given by Rev Father Prior (Marmion).

As the years passed by, Marmion found himself more and more in demand as a retreat-master. This involved constant travelling throughout Belgium, France, England and Ireland. Long before his books were published (1917 on), he had become a well-known figure in many European countries. Among those who later testified about their appreciation of these retreats, Mother Berchmans, of Hayward's Heath, England, was the most eloquent: 'I felt myself in the presence of a man of God, totally steeped in the supernatural.' The annals of many convents, in which Marmion preached retreats, give clear proof of how much this particular apostolate was appreciated.

Throughout his years in Louvain, Marmion undertook the spiritual direction of a great number of religious men and women. He did not go out of his way to seek any particular community, but rather accepted this work from the hand of God. As time went on he became involved in a number of particular communities, and committed himself to helping them. He took his work very seriously, believing that:

> The director is the instrument of Jesus Christ. The more he is united with Him, the more he renounces his own will to follow in everything the inspiration of Jesus Christ, the more efficacious will be his ministry. For my part, I will try to act in absolute dependence on Jesus Christ.

People came to him for advice, believing that he could help them in their spiritual lives. Among the individuals who came to Marmion for spiritual direction was Mgr Mercier – the future cardinal. At the time (1899-1906), Mgr Mercier was President of the Institut Supérieur de Philosophie in Louvain. They had met originally in Ireland, in 1895, at the centenary celebrations at St Patrick's College, Maynooth. Undoubtedly there was much common ground between the two men, especially their appreciation of the works of St Thomas Aquinas. They formed a friendship which lasted up to the death of Marmion in 1923. In 1906, when Mercier was appointed Archbishop of Malines, about twenty miles from Louvain, Marmion expected that their relationship as spiritual director and penitent would cease. But in fact, even when he was made cardinal in 1907, Mercier continued to seek spiritual advice from the Prior of Mont César. Furthermore, the cardinal sought to have Marmion accompany him during his annual retreats. Thus in October 1908, Mercier and Marmion made a retreat in the Benedictine Abbey of Maria Laach, Germany, and in March 1909 they went to the famous shrine of Our Lady at Paray-le-Monial. Marmion never boasted about this close relationship which he had with Cardinal Mercier, and in fact destroyed all the correspondence of a confidential nature which he had with the cardinal. In all his contacts with people, Marmion saw himself as an instrument of God, ready to share with them his own inner supernatural force. One of his spiritual sons, D. Idesbald Ryelandt, summed up Marmion's secret as a spiritual director:

> This supernatural gift allowed him to communicate to others something of the faith in Christ, which he carried within him.

Sharing his faith

Marmion was not satisfied with sharing his Christian faith with Catholics. He also believed that he had a duty, if not a mission, towards other Christians, especially Protestants. During his time in Louvain, he received a considerable number of people into the Catholic Church. Most of them were English. The first such 'convert' was a young English jockey, whom he baptised 'conditionally' on 14 June 1890. The jockey had fallen in love with a young Catholic woman, who said she would only marry him if he became a Catholic. A mutual friend introduced the jockey to Marmion. The latter immediately accepted him for instruction, and eventually received him into the Church. On 23 December 1900, Marmion received another English Protestant into the Catholic Church. The Annals of Mont César mention several such conversions in which Marmion was involved during his time in Louvain.

The most extraordinary case of conversion with which Marmion was associated, must be that of Violet Susman, a Jewess. Born in 1892, in South Africa, of wealthy parents, she was sent to school in Belgium in 1905 to learn French. While there she became gravely ill and was sent to a hospital in Louvain, where she remained for three years, hovering between life and death. One of the nuns in the hospital introduced her to Marmion, then Prior of Mont César. Some time before becoming ill, Violet Susman had seriously considered becoming a Catholic and had discussed the matter with her parents, who opposed such a step. Marmion realised from the first meeting with Violet that he was in the presence of a remarkable young girl, who was deeply religious and greatly favoured by God. According to her own Testimony, written at the request of Marmion, she had from an early age been filled with a longing for God's love. But she failed to find the necessary means of giving herself completely to God as a Jewess. While at the convent school, and especially in the hospital in Louvain, she realised that the Catholic Church would provide her with all the helps she needed to love God. However, Marmion refused to baptise her, because of her father's opposition. It was only when Violet became very ill and in danger of death, that Marmion decided to baptise her. It was Tuesday of Holy Week 1907. She described the moment as follows:

> At 2 o'clock on Tuesday in Holy Week 1907, I was baptised and became a child of the Catholic Church. I took the names of Mary Agnes. I cannot express the joy and happiness I felt. Maundy Thursday, I received my First Communion ... The following week, Mgr Mercier confirmed me and I received the seven gifts of the Holy Ghost.

Marmion kept in close touch with Violet during these difficult days, when it seemed that she could not live much longer. He had already arranged for her to become an oblate of St Benedict, and wrote to the Abbot Primate (de Hemptinne) on 9 January 1908, explaining the situation:

> I had the happiness last March to receive into the church a young Jewess and, with your permission, I received her as an oblate of St Benedict. Her noviceship should end on 16 April, but she is dying and I don't think she can live more than a few weeks now. I should be very grateful if you would authorise me to anticipate her profession, if necessary. She is a most beautiful soul, pure as an angel and in continual suffering, so as not to have more than about a half-hour's sleep in twenty-four. The light and union to which God has admitted her are surprising.

However, Violet did not die. In fact, she outlived Marmion by many years. He continued to keep in touch with her and the Susman family. Violet's mother died in South Africa, and Mr

Susman decided to move to England. He had become reconciled to the fact that his daughter had become a Catholic, and in 1918 he was received into the Catholic Church.

Such examples of 'conversions', worked through the personal intervention of Marmion, could be multiplied. As D. Idesbald Ryelandt said, when giving evidence in 1957 to the Diocesan Enquiry in Namur: 'He loved to spread the faith, and he did it with all his heart'. In another chapter, it will be necessary to deal with his involvement in the conversion of the monks of Caldey, which occurred in 1913.

First illness and last days in Louvain
Towards the end of October 1906, Marmion became ill. Since his arrival in Louvain, he had put on considerable weight, a condition further accentuated through lack of exercise. The problem was diagnosed as a 'hernia', which in those days was thought to be serious, and involved a painful operation. He wrote on 5 October 1906 to Mother Berchmans Durrant:

> I shall have to undergo an operation for rupture this month. Please pray that all may go well.

However, it was another five weeks before he went into hospital, as he told the same correspondent:

> I have just finished my retreat and I am worn out, but I must send you one line before going to bed. I go to the Institut (Dogniaux) Monday 12 November. I expect the operation for the 13th or 14th.

By 29 November, he had recovered sufficiently to write an account of his experiences in hospital:

> All danger, and, I may say, all suffering is now past. I am to get up tomorrow, and perhaps say Holy Mass on Sunday.

It took him nearly two months to recover fully from the effects of the operation. He was only 48 years of age and had another 17 years to live.

Abbot Hildebrand was particularly interested in the health of the Prior of Mont César. By 1907, he was thinking of resigning as Abbot of Maredsous and taking up permanent residence in Rome, where he held the dual office of Abbot Primate of the Benedictine Order, and Abbot of Sant' Anselmo. He had already given serious thought as to who should succeed him as Abbot of Maredsous. From all the evidence available, his firm choice was none other than Marmion. As will be shown in the following chapter, more than twice during his years in Louvain, 1905 and 1907, Marmion found himself confronted with the possibility of becoming Abbot of Maredsous. It was, however, not until 1909 that the matter was finally decided, with the resignation of Abbot Hildebrand as Abbot of Maredsous, and the election of Marmion as his successor.

Part II

Abbot of Maredsous, c. 1912

CHAPTER 5

Election as Abbot of Maredsous
in 1909

The Benedictine monastery of Maredsous had been founded in 1872. For its first six years, it remained a priory, ruled over by D. Placide Wolter, a German, from the mother-house Beuron. In 1878, it was raised to the status of an abbey, and D. Placide Wolter became the first Abbot of Maredsous. He ruled the monastery until 1890, when he was elected Archabbot of Beuron, in succession to his brother, D. Maur Wolter, who had died. It was during the abbacy of D. Placide Wolter, that Marmion entered Maredsous in 1886.

In 1890, D. Hildebrand de Hemptinne, a Belgian, was elected second Abbot of Maredsous, a position he held until his resignation in 1909. By any standard, Abbot Hildebrand was a very remarkable man. He had been one of the principal actors in the foundation of Maredsous. Before being elected Abbot of Maredsous, he had served as novice-master in Beuron, then as prior of the English foundation made by Beuron, at Erdington, near Birmingham, and finally as secretary to Archabbot Maur Wolter in Beuron. He was still a monk of Beuron when elected Abbot of Maredsous, in August 1890. One of his most obvious assets was the fact that he spoke fluent French, German, English and Italian. Under such a leader, the future of Maredsous was guaranteed and, indeed, it prospered beyond all expectations. However, from the very beginning, there was a big question mark surrounding his rule. He appeared to be more interested in what was going on in Italy, and especially in Rome, than what was happening in the Belgian scene. Within three years of his election as Abbot of Maredsous, he was appointed Abbot Primate of the Benedictine Order by Pope Leo XIII, a position which called for his almost permanent residence in Rome. Yet he continued to be Abbot of Maredsous as well for the next sixteen years.

While Abbot Hildebrand de Hemptinne could not be accused of utterly neglecting his own monastery, a great number of question marks hung over the arrangement sanctioned by Pope Leo XIII. There was no precedent for any abbot holding down three offices, and certainly no machinery at hand to monitor or enforce his retiring from any one or other of his responsibilities. The whole matter was allowed to drift along from one year to another, without any solution or decision in sight. Although the Abbot Primate did not relinquish his abbacy of Maredsous until 1909, in fact, there were two earlier moments, when it seemed that he was on the point of resigning as Abbot of Maredsous in 1905 and 1907.

The Year of Decision: 1909

Early in 1909, the first definite hint of the impending resignation of the Abbot Primate as Abbot of Maredsous, came in a letter he wrote to his sister, the Abbess of Maredret. He confided to her that he was finding it impossible:

> … to cope with all the work entailed in running Sant' Anselmo, Maredsous and the Primacy. The work is insurmountable. Here I am once again plunged in waves of letters.

He was to spend the next six months making the necessary arrangements for his resignation as Abbot of Maredsous. He also had to make certain that the man he had in mind as his successor, namely Marmion, would be ready for the job and acceptable to the community of Maredsous.

The Chapter General met in Beuron between 4-7 June 1909. Marmion attended, having been elected delegate of the community of Mont César. When the Abbot Primate brought up the question of his resigning as Abbot of Maredsous, no immediate solution was proposed, apart from the suggestion that a Canonical Visitation of Maredsous be undertaken in the near future. However, this visitation never took place. Instead, the Abbot Primate, having realised at long last the seriousness of the situation, wrote on 1 August 1909 to Pope Pius X, offering his resignation as Abbot of Maredsous. The pope replied on 4 August 1909, expressing the wish that Abbot Hildebrand should leave Maredsous, and come to live permanently in Rome, as Abbot Primate and Abbot of Sant' Anselmo.

Thus the ground was now prepared for an election in Maredsous.

The month of August 1909 saw feverish discussions and rumours circulating in the corridors of Maredsous, regarding possible candidates to succeed to Abbot Hildebrand. From a study of all the available documents, it seems clear that the community were seeking a man with certain qualities. First of all, they wanted someone who had experience as a spiritual guide and leader. Secondly, they were looking for someone capable of restoring the spiritual equilibrium of the monastery. They were not looking for an administrator, but for a spiritual father. The one man who seemed to fit this bill, was D. Columba Marmion, the Prior of Mont César, though a monk of Maredsous by profession. He would be one of the front runners in the contest.

Abbot Primate de Hemptinne had foreseen one obstacle to Marmion's being elected Abbot of Maredsous, namely the fact that he was a citizen of the United Kingdom of England and Ireland. However, this matter was taken in hand in June 1909, when Marmion was advised by the Abbot Primate to renounce his British citizenship and become a naturalised Belgian. It was a step he would hardly have taken all by himself, seeing his deep Irish patriotism, and was a sign that he had now committed himself to Belgium and the Belgians.

Abbot Primate de Hemptinne made one final arrangement, which was to increase the chances of Marmion being elected his successor in Maredsous. He chose Marmion to give the annual retreat to the community of Maredsous, held that year from 12-19 September, a mere ten days or so before the election. This was an astute move on the part of the Abbot Primate, who was aware of Marmion's special charism for giving retreats and winning the hearts and minds of his audience.

The Election: 28 September 1909
When the retreat was over, on 18 September, Marmion returned immediately to Louvain. The next day, Abbot Primate de Hemptinne, who had not attended the retreat, made a formal announcement to the assembled community in Maredsous, that he had decided to resign as their abbot. He had already given a clear hint of this in a conference to the community on 26 May 1909, but the community had no definite word about the matter until 19 September. In a lengthy discourse, he traced the history of his abbacy over the past nineteen years (1890-1909), and especially since his appointment as Abbot Primate. This discourse

was his 'Swan Song' as Abbot of Maredsous, an emotional moment for himself and his community. He then handed over all
his powers as Abbot of Maredsous to the prior, D. Basile de
Meester, who would retain full responsibility until the election
of the new abbot.

The election of the new abbot took place on 28 September 1909,
under the presidency of the Archabbot of Beuron, D. Ildefonse
Schober. D. Columba Marmion was elected on the second scrutiny,
receiving 46 out of a total electorate of 66. Immediately after the
result was verified, two delegates, DD. Jules Jonckeere and
Grégoire Fournier, were dispatched to Mont César, to announce
the news to the newly elected Abbot of Maredsous. They arrived
that same evening, 28 September.

As soon as he heard the news of his election, Marmion went to
see his abbot, D. Robert de Kerchove, to ask permission to accept
the honour now offered him. It appears that Abbot Robert had
decided, at the last moment, not to exercise his veto. Thus, it was
with some surprise that, when Marmion approached Abbot
Robert, the latter not only agreed to his prior accepting the abbacy
of Maredsous, but actually ordered Marmion, under obedience
to accept it.

Marmion did not have much time for farewells, as he had to
leave Louvain for Maredsous that same morning of 29
September. After ten years in Mont César, he had become attached to the place. He had made many friends among the community of Mont César, where he was held in high honour. At the
same time, he had made many friends among the people of
Louvain, who would miss him. Finally, he had been chaplain to
the Carmelite Sisters in Louvain since leaving Maredsous in
1899, and had formed a special relationship with M. Marie-
Joseph van Arden, the prioress, and other members of the community. It was a nostalgic moment for him, and not least his
having to say farewell to Abbot Robert de Kerchove. They had
worked together as a team for ten years, and helped to build up
a strong and united community. Abbot Robert was not at all
pleased to part with his prior. The Annals of Mont César give a
rather laconic and brief reference to the honour bestowed on
Marmion:

> We have heard of the election of D. Columba Marmion as
> Abbot of Maredsous. This is no small sacrifice for Abbot

Robert, to part with his Prior, who had been his devoted helper since the first days of our monastery.

However, Abbot Robert gave a more generous account of how he agreed to the appointment of his prior, when writing to D. Cécile de Hemptinne on 30 September 1909.

They have just taken away my Prior. I did all I could to hold on to him, but once it appeared that such was the will of God, I gave in.

Abbatial Blessing, 3 October 1909

When Marmion arrived in Maredsous from Louvain on the morning of Wednesday 29 September, the bells of the abbey church rang out a welcome. He was then led to the Chapter room and asked by Archabbot Schober if he accepted his election and consented to it. Marmion replied in a firm voice: 'I obey and accept the will of God'. Archabbot Schober then handed over to Marmion the keys of the church and the seal of the monastery, emblems of his jurisdiction and authority. Then the newly elected abbot was given the pectoral cross, a symbol of the heavy burden he was taking on his shoulders. Finally, sitting in the abbot's stall in choir, he received a promise of obedience 'until death' from all his monks.

The following day, Marmion left Maredsous, to spend three days in retreat in the country villa belonging to his friend, Cardinal Mercier. There he prepared himself for the solemn abbatial blessing, which was to take place in Maredsous on Sunday 3 October 1909, the Feast of the Holy Rosary. He had expressed a wish to be blessed by Abbot Primate de Hemptinne, and by a special papal privilege this was arranged. The assistant-abbots were D. Robert de Kerchove of Mont César, and D. Fidelis von Stotzingen of Maria Laach. Archabbot Schober, and many of the Belgian and German abbots of the Beuronese Congregation, were also present. In addition, a great number of friends had come from Louvain, to honour the former Prior of Mont César. Among these were Mgr Ladeuze, the Rector Magnificus of the University of Louvain, and Mgr Becker, the Rector of the American College. Dr Matthew Marmion, the new abbot's brother, had come from Ireland to represent the Marmion family.

After the ceremony, the new abbot, wearing the mitre and carrying his crozier, walked around the church, giving his blessing to the congregation. Then all the invited guests adjourned to the monastery refectory which was suitably decorated for the occasion and included a large banner with Marmion's motto written in bold lettering: *Magis prodesse quam praeesse* ('Better to serve than to command').

Although Marmion's career as an abbot seemed to begin on a triumphant note, in fact, he found it all very humbling. He knew that his life would change dramatically, but as in the past, he relied on his faith and his prayer-life to see him through. His election as Abbot of Maredsous did not change him in any way, at least in regard to his interior life. He had nearly fourteen years of hard labour ahead of him, which in time would take its toll of his energy and strength. But on that lovely October day in 1909, the future lay in front of him, like an uncharted sea, on which he had to guide his monastic ship and its crew into a safe harbour.

CHAPTER 6

First Years as Abbot
(1909-1912)

Settling in as abbot

One of the first reports we get of the new Abbot of Maredsous, is in a letter he wrote to his friend, Mother Peter Garnier, of Tyburn Convent, London, on 12 October 1909, in which he said that he was keeping well and that:

> everyone is so good to me ... Next Friday (15 October), I sing my first pontifical Mass.

Ten days later, he wrote to the Abbot Primate, Hildebrand de Hemptinne:

> Today, I breathe for the first time. Up to now I have been so busy that my every moment was taken up. The community shows itself very well disposed towards me. It is an accepted fact that it will never be possible to fill the void left by your departure. However, everyone makes allowances for my insufficiency and my good will.

The Benedictine Sisters of Maredret kept a close eye on the newly elected Abbot of Maredsous, who was an old friend. Their Annals give almost daily bulletins of the 'happenings' in Maredsous, during the month of October 1909. They awaited anxiously his first visit. Their abbess, D. Cécile de Hemptinne, felt it her duty to write to her brother, the Abbot Primate, on 27 October 1909, to tell him:

> The new Abbot is somewhat overcome by the work. He intends to interest himself in the least details. His health is very good. I believe that, in general, all are very happy with him.

It is quite true that Marmion was 'somewhat overcome by the work.' He gave a full picture of his busy daily schedule to Mother Stanislaus, of the English Convent, Bruges, in a letter at the end of October 1909:

The administration of this monastery, with its numerous community (130), its College, its school of art, its farm, and St Scholastica (Maredret), would take up the time of an abbot in any ordinary time, especially if, as I try to do, he is present at all the Divine Office ... Our Lord has helped me wonderfully up to this. All hearts are inclined towards me, so that I meet nothing but docility and good will.

Less than a month after his abbatial blessing, Marmion had to interrupt his letter-writing and other work, to preach the annual retreat to the staff and students of the College of the Holy Spirit in Louvain. This was the first of many such exits he would make in the years ahead, to preach retreats not only in Belgium, but in England, Ireland and France. His pastoral heart embraced everyone, and made him respond positively to calls for help and spiritual guidance, from both inside and outside the monastery. He seemed to thrive on any work which allowed him to exercise his priestly and monastic ministry, as he told one correspondent on 12 December 1909:

I must confess that, up to this, things have been much easier than I had anticipated. I see more and more that the great point is to sink our personality and let Christ act in us and through us.

By Christmas 1909, Marmion had settled in to the daily routine of running a large Benedictine abbey. Most of his decisions concerned internal matters: which of his student monks should be sent to Rome or Louvain for their studies; which of his monks should be asked to teach in either the Secondary or Arts School; who should be director of the *Revue Bénédictine* and the *Messager de S. Benoît*; who should be admitted to simple or solemn profession, or allowed to proceed to ordination, and so on. However, the Abbot of Maredsous was soon to be faced with making greater decisions, which concerned matters of both external and internal interest.

Background to the Katanga affair

The Belgian people, ever since the foundation of the state in 1831, have had a very close association with the royal family, and never more so than at the turn of the century. Léopold II (1835-1909), King of the Belgians, had become sovereign of the Congo in 1885, and in 1908 the Congo had become a Belgian colony. This African colony brought great wealth, as well as many benefits, to Belgium. Then, quite unexpectedly, on 17 December 1909, Léopold II, who had reigned since 1865, died and the country was thrown into a period of national mourning. Maredsous could not allow itself to be outside the mainstream of devotion to their dead sovereign. On the advice of his Council, Marmion went to Brussels to represent his community at the funeral of the king, which took place on 22 December 1909. The following day, 23 December, Marmion officiated at a Pontifical Requiem Mass for the late king in the abbey church of Maredsous, which was attended by a large congregation. That same day, Albert I (1875-1934) was proclaimed the new king. Thus the end of the year 1909 ushered in a new era in Belgium, as it did in Maredsous. And by a strange coincidence, Maredsous and the Belgian government were to become involved that same year, in what became known as 'The Katanga Affair'.

Early in December 1909, the Abbot of Maredsous received an official request from the Belgian government, to make a monastic foundation in Katanga, which was part of the Belgian Congo. Marmion wrote immediately to the Abbot Primate:

> An official of the Colonial Ministry is to come here next week, to put forward a proposal that we make a foundation in the Congo. I am inclined to accept the foundation in principle. Here in Maredsous, everyone is enthusiastic.

At this stage, Marmion was simply passing on information, but was not yet in a position to give any specific details of the government's offer. He was also unaware that the Abbot Primate – then Abbot of Maredsous – had been approached with a similar offer thirteen years previously, in 1896, and had turned it down, owing to a commitment to a similar mission in Brazil at the time. However, at the same time as he declined the government's offer, the Abbot Primate, in a letter dated 8 December 1896, gave a veiled promise of taking up the offer at a later date. The following are the actual words of the former Abbot of Maredsous, D. Hildebrand de Hemptinne:

> We in Maredsous have several times considered the possibility of making a foundation in the Congo, in order to show our great admiration for the work undertaken by His Majesty. ... Unfortunately, our good will cannot at this mo-

ment be realised, because the Holy See has just given us charge of Brazil ... We would, however, hope some day to take up this matter, and thus accede to the wishes of His Majesty.

However, no further request had come from the Belgian government to Maredsous, until the one now made to Marmion in December 1909.

First Approaches by the Belgian Government
Jules Renkin, the Belgian government Minister for the Colonies in 1909, had a genuine interest in bringing the benefits of European civilisation to the Congo. He hoped to use Belgian Catholic missionaries as part of this civilising plan. One long-standing proposal of the Belgian government was the foundation of an abbey, in the purely medieval tradition, to be set up in the Congo, to counteract the growing English Protestant influence. He instructed his Director General, Edouard Kervyn, to examine the situation. The latter first of all approached a Belgian Missionary Society, 'Les Pères de Scheut,' but they turned down the offer. Secondly, he approached the Belgian Trappists, but they likewise were not interested. Thus Maredsous was the third choice, and every effort was made to guarantee its success.

Edouard Kervyn arranged to visit Maredsous over the Christmas holidays of 1909 to discuss his government's proposals with the monks of Maredsous. He stayed three days in the monastery, and had lengthy discussions with D. Hubert Casier, D. Grégoire Fournier, and Marmion himself. He explained that the government planned to found a Benedictine abbey on the high plateaux of Katanga. The land (2000 hectares) would be offered by the government free of charge, and in addition 200,000 francs would be given to the community in 1910, and 100,000 francs in 1911. After these preliminary talks with the abbot and the two members of the community, Kervyn seemed to be pleased and made a note to the effect that:

> There is reason to believe that the Benedictines will accept the offer to found a large abbey in Katanga. In principle, the idea has met with the approval of the three dignitaries I discussed it with, and also a large number of the monks.

Marmion realised that this offer presented him with his first great challenge as Abbot of Maredsous. He had always been a missionary at heart, and here was a chance to involve himself with missionary work at first hand. He also had to face up to the fact that there was a patriotic side to the offer. He had to avoid acting in a way which might appear unpatriotic. The fact that he was a foreigner left him in a delicate position. In order to avoid falling into any error of judgement, Marmion felt it his duty to consult both the Archabbot of Beuron and the Abbot Primate.

He explained the delicate situation in a letter to Archabbot Schober on 28 December 1909:

> As the work is a national and patriotic undertaking, I must be very careful not to oppose it. It will only mean supplying 3 or 4 monks to begin with, and as the conditions offered by the government are so good, and as we have many vocations this year, I am inclined to accept the foundation.

At the same time, Marmion instructed one of his monks, D. Grégoire Fournier, to write at greater length to the archabbot, giving a full account of the government's proposals. After giving a fairly glowing report of the site for the proposed monastery in Katanga, D. Grégoire concluded with these words:

> Father Abbot Columba told the official sent by the Minister of the Colonies, that if the Abbot Primate and the Archabbot of Beuron gave their favourable opinion, he would accept the proposals made by the Belgian Government. A refusal by Maredsous would give a bad impression in Belgium, whereas an acceptance would be considered very favourably by everyone.

Not satisfied with all these explanations, Marmion decided to write a second letter himself to the archabbot, dated 6 January 1910, in which he said:

> My intention would be to make a foundation completely Beuronese in character. I would accept no vocations (here in Maredsous) for the missions, but simply to be a monk. Then the Abbot could choose freely those that he would send to the Congo.

Under six headings, he summarised the various points at issue, insisting that:

> If we do not accept, the refusal will be attributed to the Abbot of Maredsous, who is not a Belgian. Furthermore, we must

come to a decision immediately. Personally, I am indifferent. I would prefer, in fact, that this question did not arise just now. Yet, I would be reluctant to refuse. However, I only wish to do what God wills, and I shall let myself be guided by your advice.

Opposition of Archabbot Schober

Archabbot Schober replied in a long letter, in which he pointed out the difficulties and objections to the Congo foundation. He evidently looked at the problem purely from the Beuronese point of view, and his main objection was couched in the following words:

What is really the essential factor, is to know if, in the Congo, you could create an abbey entirely in the spirit and according to the Constitutions of our Congregation. If this is not possible, one could on no account enter into any negotiations, and it would be necessary to decline the offer.

The archabbot also reminded Marmion that Maredsous already had too many responsibilities. At the last Chapter General of the Beuronese Congregation, Maredsous was made responsible for the Portuguese abbey of Cucujaes, which was in great difficulties. On top of this, there was the mission to Brazil, the Louvain House of Studies (Mont César), two schools, two reviews, numerous retreats to be preached, etc. The archabbot's final and most telling point was the question of lay-brothers. A large number would be needed for the foundation, but Maredsous had always been short of them and there was little or no hope of recruiting any lay-brothers among the Congolese.

The archabbot's letter, therefore, contained a great number of reservations, and reflected his apprehension over the proposed missionary endeavour, as proposed by the Belgian government. He was, in fact, reiterating a resolution passed by the Chapter General of the Beuronese Congregation in 1891, which disapproved of any missionary foundation being undertaken by an individual monastery. The abbots had proposed the establishing of a monastery, belonging to the Beuronese Congregation, which would be given specific charge of any future missionary effort. If Marmion were to go ahead with the missionary foundation in Katanga, he would be contravening the injunctions of the Chapter General. The archabbot threw more shadows than light on the question, and undoubtedly had a very considerable influence in turning many of the monks of Maredsous against the Katanga enterprise. But before he could make up his mind, Marmion had to await the reply from the Abbot Primate.

The Abbot Primate offers his advice

The Abbot Primate (D. Hildebrand de Hemptinne) received no less than five letters from Maredsous, telling him of the Belgian government's offer. Two of these were written by Marmion, while the other three – written at the request of the Abbot of Maredsous – were from D. Hubert Casier. They all made the same appeal to the Abbot Primate, to give his personal opinion on the Katanga foundation. However, he found it difficult to come up with any clear-cut solution, as he explained to his sister, D. Cécile de Hemptinne, the Abbess of Maredret:

> I have not yet replied to the Abbot of Maredsous on the subject of the Congo, because it is a very serious matter, both from the theoretical and practical point of view. I have to be all the more prudent, since I realise the great weight which will be attached to my reply. Pray and have prayers said that the Holy Spirit may enlighten me.

It was only on 4 February that the Abbot Primate finally put pen to paper to reply to Marmion, and what he said was somewhat inconclusive:

> I am inclined to give the government an affirmative reply, and for this reason: To withdraw in the present circumstances would be more embarrassing than to have to withdraw later. At least we would have proved our good will, if we fail. But my honest advice would be for you to ask the government to give us at least until Easter to make a final decision.

Such advice was not very helpful, being over-cautious and half-hearted in its message. Considering Abbot de Hemptinne's views on the Congo, as expressed in his letter of 1896, this present letter was almost a volte-face.

On the other hand, the Abbot Primate knew that the proposal was capable of another solution, although it would take time to get it off the ground. This other solution concerned two monks of Maredsous, who had been assigned to missionary work in Brazil, but had recently been released from that mission, namely, D. Gérard van Caloen and D. Jean de Hemptinne. They might easily be diverted to the Katanga foundation. In fact, van

Caloen, realising that the Brazil mission was a failure, was already on his way back to Europe and was thinking of offering himself for the Congo mission. The Abbot Primate hoped to sort out all these matters at a General Chapter of the Brazilian Benedictines to be held in Rome in March 1910. He would await the outcome of this before deciding anything. Thus, in his own mind, the Abbot Primate had not completely closed the door on a foundation in Katanga, with some Maredsous monks involved.

A major stumbling-block

When Edouard Kervyn visited Maredsous at the end of December 1909, he had received a promise from Marmion that an answer would be given to the government within fifteen days. However, owing to the delay in receiving an answer from the Abbot Primate, it was impossible for the Abbot of Maredsous to give any such definite reply.

It must also be said that time was running out for Edouard Kervyn, who, as delegate of the Minister for the Colonies, was obliged to know as soon as possible if Maredsous was going to make a foundation. Indeed, a government-sponsored expedition was about to set off in March for Katanga to do a survey of the country and seek out a suitable site for the proposed Benedictine abbey. Edouard Kervyn wrote to D. Hubert Casier on 19 January 1910, asking if any decision had been reached by the monks of Maredsous. D. Hubert Casier replied to Kervyn the following day:

> I can quite understand your impatience to get a final word (on the Katanga project). Here is the reason for the delay: Several of the monks are full of enthusiasm, but others are afraid of the risks involved in the adventure.

There were other reasons for the delay on the part of the Abbot of Maredsous and his community. They did not wish to be hurried into making a decision, and were somewhat shocked at the precipitation on the part of the government. Time was needed to explore all the aspects of the case. Certainly they would need more than two weeks to decide such an important matter. The normal procedure would be for the Abbot of Maredsous to send two monks to Katanga to investigate the site and report back to the community. This, however, was not possible, given the government's time schedule.

It was also at this stage – January and February 1910 – that a new difficulty arose. It became more and more evident that the government envisaged the Benedictines involving themselves in the agricultural scene in Katanga. As the monks of Maredsous began to read the small print in the government's proposal, it was seen that there would be very little opportunity for intellectual work. The main source of income from the 2000 hectares would be agricultural produce. But the monks of Maredsous knew nothing about African climatic conditions, kinds of crops to be grown in Katanga, let alone farm management on a large scale, in the days before tractors and combine harvesters. The stumbling block lay in the phrase used over and over again by the government: colonisation by farming. D. Grégoire Fournier, who had in the beginning been in favour of the Katanga proposal, was one of the first to recognise this factor of 'an agricultural foundation.' He thought the whole enterprise beyond the resources or possibility of the monks of Maredsous.

The Abbot of Maredsous sought the advice from people who knew the African scene and were *au fait* with the problems of farming there. One report was sent to Marmion, which painted a grim picture of agricultural problems in Katanga.

> The offer of 2000 hectares of land is grand, but more grand than useful. In Africa, such a piece of land does not mean anything, except you have money and hands enough to work it in a profitable way. In Africa, crops have to be sold and eaten within 3 months after the harvest. If you stock them up longer than that time, the bark-worm destroys everything.

From all sides came the same advice: The offer made by the government would not really suffice for the foundation and maintenance of a Benedictine abbey in the Congo.

Marmion calls a Chapter Meeting, 11 February 1910
A few days after he received the letter, dated 4 February 1910, from the Abbot Primate, Marmion decided to call a full Chapter meeting in Maredsous. He did so for two good reasons. Firstly, he felt it his duty to consult the Chapter and get their views on the Katanga proposal. The matter was already public, and was a topic of daily conversation in Maredsous. People were taking sides, and the whole affair was causing considerable anxiety, and even division, in the community. Secondly, his reply to the

Belgian government was long overdue. He does not seem to have considered acting on the advice of the Abbot Primate 'to ask the government for a delay until Easter before giving a final answer.' For better or for worse, Marmion thought that there had been enough talking, and enough writing of letters, on the Katanga mission, and that the time had come to make a decision.

The Chapter met on 11 February, with Marmion presiding. He opened the proceedings by giving a summary of the original government offer. Then he read the long letter of the Archabbot of Beuron (11-12 Jan 1910), with its telling phrase: 'The foundation should not be undertaken, unless it be guaranteed a real monastic character in the Beuronese tradition, with an abbot and twelve monks. Without these, it would simply be a mission-station, and not an abbey.' These words of the archabbot made a considerable impression on the members of the Chapter.

Finally, after all had given their views, the matter was put to the vote. There were 32 votes against accepting the government's offer, and only 6 in favour. Thus the Abbot of Maredsous had a clear mandate for giving a firm 'No' to the government. However, he still hesitated to give the final word of refusal, until he had communicated with the Abbot Primate. He wrote to the latter on 13 February 1910, announcing the negative vote, explaining how it had come about:

> Despite the enthusiasm of all the community for the foundation, which appeared so patriotic, so important for the glory of God and of souls, yet almost all were strongly opposed in practice, because of our limitations of personnel. I have decided nothing as yet, but will await your advice, taking into account the attitude and the desires of the community, who have voted 32 against the foundation, and 6 for.

The Abbot Primate wrote back on 17 February, saying that:

> After the Chapter decision of 11 February, and the negative vote in regard to the foundation in Katanga, you can hardly go back on the matter, without exposing yourself to serious inconveniences. It will be necessary to inform the government and give them a negative reply.

Thus it seemed that the matter was ended. It only remained for Marmion to compose a tactful letter to the Belgian government, explaining the reasons for turning down their offer. It proved to be one of the most difficult letters he ever wrote, as he really wished in his heart that his monks had supported the Katanga foundation.

Marmion was well aware of the repercussions, especially in Brussels and Rome, following on the decision not to take up the Katanga mission. He knew that certain interested parties, such as Mgr Gérard van Caloen, might complain him to the pope, as being too timid and failing in his responsibilities to the Catholics of the Belgian Congo. Marmion mentioned this matter to Archabbot Schober, when he wrote to inform him of the final negative answer to the Belgian government:

> In order to avoid an Apostolic mandate, I have just written a letter to the Holy Father, explaining the situation in Maredsous and the impossibility of giving any monks without damage to our schools and other works. I am convinced that it is impossible at this moment to undertake a truly Benedictine work in Katanga. It would be a failure …

There is no doubt that the Katanga affair was a useful initiation into the world of decision-making for the new Abbot of Maredsous. It was a testing-time for him, and he emerged from it a wiser man. Neither he, nor any of the monks of Maredsous, were compromised by the negotiations, and certainly that was something to be thankful for. Above all, the spiritual values of Benedictine life, as understood and practised in Maredsous at the time, were maintained and even strengthened. At the same time, one suspects that Marmion showed some degree of timidity in this first great challenge. He was, apparently, acting very much in the shadow of his predecessor, Abbot Hildebrand de Hemptinne. The latter – right up to the time of his death in 1913 – kept a close eye on Maredsous. It was only gradually that Marmion freed himself from the de Hemptinne influence. By the time the next great challenge came along, in 1913, Marmion was his own man.

CHAPTER 7

The Caldey Affair
(1913-1914)

Sometime in the year 1896, a young English medical student, Benjamin Fearnley Carlyle, set up a small community of religious men – all members of the Church of England – who called themselves 'The Oblate Brothers of the Holy Order of St Benedict.' Benjamin Carlyle changed his name to that of Brother Aelred, and appointed himself superior of the community. His intention was to revive Benedictine monastic life within the Church of England. After some years in a temporary building in East London, and then in Painsthorpe, Yorkshire, Br Aelred and his community eventually settled on Caldey Island, off the coast of South Wales, in 1906. From the very beginnings of his religious life, Br Aelred felt attracted to the Roman Catholic Church, although at the same time he maintained a strong loyalty to the Church of England. He was furthermore encouraged to remain within the Anglican fold after receiving official approval of his community from Dr Temple, the Archbishop of Canterbury. The latter gave his permission for Br Aelred and his fellow monks, to make their monastic professions and take vows. Br Aelred outlined his ideas on monastic life in a booklet called *The Benedictines of Caldey Island*, in which he says that:

> We in Caldey, in common with many others elsewhere, find our vocation to live in community under the Holy Rule of St Benedict.

The move to Caldey Island provided Br Aelred and his growing community with an ideal setting for their monastic way of life.

By then, he had assumed the title of abbot, having been ordained priest and given the abbatial blessing by Bishop Grafton of Wisconsin, USA, in 1903. The monks undertook an ambitious building programme, and eventually constructed a magnificent monastery, with a church, living quarters, guest-house, etc. By

1912, these Anglican monks had become well-known through-out the English-speaking world, mainly through their guest-house and their quarterly journal called *Pax*. As Abbot Aelred wrote in the March 1912 issue of *Pax*:

> For fourteen years, mostly passed in real obscurity and diffi-culty, we have been trying to learn to be monks ... And now, with a settled mode and a growing community, we ask noth-ing better than to hide ourselves and to keep strictly to our Rule and Cloister.

These Anglican monks were, in fact, leading a full Benedictine life. They recited the Divine Offices in choir, in the Latin lan-guage, celebrated a daily Eucharistic Service (said by Abbot Carlyle, the only priest in the community), had reservation of the Blessed Sacrament, devotions to Our Lady, and followed the Calendar of the English Congregation of the Benedictine Order, with all the Catholic feasts. Most of the spiritual books read by the monks were by Catholic authors, such as Father Baker and Abbot Blosius. However, it should be said that by 1912, the life of the Caldey monks was more Cistercian than Benedictine, at least in its externals. The monks rose at 2 am for the Night Office, they abstained from meat and laid great emphasis on manual work. They also wore a white tunic, with a black scapular, after the model of Cistercians. Abbot Aelred had worked out a monastic timetable and way of life, which he publicised in his book *Our Purpose and Method* and which evidently worked well on Caldey. As one visitor to Caldey wrote:

> In everything Catholic they are one with us, except that de-plorable fact, they are not in communion with the Sovereign Pontiff and the Apostolic See of Rome.

He noted:

> ... the monk's devotion to Our Lady, the beauty of the singing, the magnificent vestments and the firm, but gentle rule of the Abbot.

One might, indeed, ask why it took so long for the community of Anglican Benedictine monks to make the decision to seek full communion with Rome. One answer which has been given sug-gests that Abbot Aelred and his monks were so absorbed in surviving (their economic position was always rather tenuous), and in building their new monastery (it was only completed in 1912), that they had little or no time to study their situation.

The Crisis of Identity, 1912-1913

On 6 March 1912, Abbot Aelred had an interview in Lambeth Palace with Dr Davidson, the Archbishop of Canterbury. He hoped to solve some of his difficulties in regard to his own ecclesiastical standing, and that of his community in Caldey. However, the Archbishop of Canterbury offered no immediate solution, but suggested an episcopal visitation as a preliminary to making any final decision. The man chosen to conduct the visitation was Dr Gore, Bishop of Oxford. There followed a lengthy correspondence between Abbot Aelred and Bishop Gore, as the latter was unable to visit Caldey that year (1912). Bishop Gore requested that Abbot Aelred send him a copy of the Constitutions of Caldey, and was surprised to find how un-Anglican these were. One particular section in the Constitution was found quite unacceptable, relating to a 'return to the External Unity of the whole Church, and communion with the Holy See of Rome.'

On 8 February 1913, having examined the various documents sent him by Abbot Aelred, Bishop Gore wrote to the latter, making it quite clear that he had very considerable reservations about the authenticity of the way of life of the Caldey monks under the Church of England laws. He concluded that unless the Caldey monks were prepared to change their ways radically, there could be no 'possibility of bargaining and concession.' This letter came like a bombshell to Abbot Aelred. He decided, therefore, to call a community meeting, and gave each member a copy of the bishop's letter. He then asked each of the brethren whether the time had come to break with the Church of England and go over to Rome. He added that, as far as he was concerned, he had no alternative but to submit to the Roman Catholic Church. It was found that nearly all the brethren had reached the same decision as their abbot. On 19 February 1913, Abbot Aelred wrote a letter to Bishop Gore, which was signed by twenty-seven monks, out of total community of thirty-three, saying that:

> … as a Community, we cannot conscientiously submit to the demands you make of us.

In a final letter to Bishop Gore, dated 22 February 1913, Abbot Aelred stated that:

> … our conclusion is that we are thrown back upon the strictly Papal basis of authority, and we intend at once making our submission to Rome.

The same day, Abbot Aelred, who at that moment decided to cease acting as a priest in the Church of England, sent a telegram to Dr Mostyn, the Catholic bishop of Minevia, in whose diocese Caldey Island lay, explaining the whole situation. He sent another telegram to his old friend, D. Bede Camm, a monk of Maredsous, begging him to come to Caldey as soon as possible to help and advise him. He followed up this telegram to D. Bede Camm with a letter, begging him:

> ... to give us the benefit of your help and advice with regard to our reception into the Catholic Church.

Marmion becomes involved in Caldey, March 1913
The year 1913 opened for Marmion with a journey to England, to preach the annual retreat to the Benedictine monks of Erdington Abbey, Birmingham. He returned in time to celebrate the Silver Jubilee of his monastic profession on 10th February. Thus he was in Maredsous when Abbot Aelred's telegram and letter arrived, asking D. Bede Camm to help the Caldey community. Marmion immediately gave his permission to D. Bede to undertake this mission, and the latter arrived in Caldey on 25 February 1913. He was greatly impressed with the situation there, but felt he needed help in preparing the community of Anglican monks for their reception into the Catholic Church. He thus decided to ask Marmion to come to Caldey, and the Abbot of Maredsous arrived in Caldey on 3 March.

Marmion gave a number of Conferences to the Caldey monks. He chose as his text for the first Conference the words of Psalm 149: 'Sing to the Lord a new song; the praise of the Lord is celebrated in the Church of the Saints.' He made an indelible impression on his hearers, who saw Marmion as representing the authentic voice of Benedictine monasticism.

It was a most unusual affair. The Abbot of Maredsous was caught up in the general enthusiasm which filled all Roman Catholics in England on receiving news of the events in Caldey. The matter had been brought to the notice of Pope Pius X, who instructed his Secretary of State, Cardinal Merry del Val, to dispatch the following telegram to D. Bede Camm, dated 2 March 1913:

> Holy Father affectionately blesses new converts on their reception into the fold, and prays God to grant them the

abundance of every grace. Please express to each and everyone of both communities my deepest the most affectionate
sympathy.

Bishop Mostyn of Menevia, in whose diocese Caldey Island was,
took an immediate interest in the newly converted community.
He was eventually given full jurisdiction by Rome over them.
The Caldey annalist describes in the following words, the memorable ceremony which took place on 5 March 1913:

> The community made its formal submission to the Catholic
> Church. Kneeling around Fr Abbot Aelred, in the middle of
> the choir, they made their profession of faith in the Catholic
> Church and her creeds, and the abjuration of heresy and
> schism, in the presence of the Bishop (Mostyn), seated before
> the altar.

The monks who had submitted to Rome were now in an anom-
alous situation as their vows had no ecclesiastical status under
Roman canon law. Furthermore, there was no precedent to indicate what should be done with them. It was at this stage that
Marmion stepped in to offer a practical solution. His proposal –
which eventually met with approval from Bishop Mostyn, the
Abbot Primate of the Benedictine Order and the Roman Congregation for Religious – was a simple one, namely that all the
monks of Caldey, including Abbot Aelred, should be made secular oblates of Maredsous. This would give them some kind of
corporate monastic existence, until such time as they made profession, following a canonical novitiate. In addition, Marmion
proposed that Abbot Aelred would do his novitiate and priestly
studies in Maredsous, and that he (Marmion) would take personal responsibility for everything relating to such an agreement. The rest of the community would remain in Caldey.
Marmion offered two monks of Maredsous, both English and
former Anglicans, to help in Caldey during the transition period.
This arrangement was agreed on by all parties, and the two
Maredsous monks were officially appointed: D. John Chapman,
to act as temporary superior, and D. Bede Camm, as novice-
master. Reflecting on the role which the Abbot of Maredsous
played in Caldey at this stage, D. Bede Camm wrote on 15
March 1913:

> No one can say how kind and splendid he (Marmion) has
> been! He has won everyone's heart completely.

Marmion showed how pleased he was with the whole proceedings, when he wrote on 17 March 1913 to the Abbot Primate Hildebrand de Hemptinne, giving him an account of the Caldey 'conversions'.

It was also agreed between Bishop Mostyn, the Abbot of Maredsous and Abbot Gasquet that nothing of the ordinary monastic life in Caldey should be changed. However, the Caldey situation had to be cleared with Rome, and Bishop Mostyn asked Marmion to take care of this matter. Marmion wrote to the Congregation for Religious, asking them to underwrite all the decisions and arrangements made for the Caldey converts. He was pleased to find that he got all the support and more than he expected as he explained in a letter to D. Bede Camm on 16 June 1913:

> Just a line to enclose copy of the documents received from the Congregation for Religious. I have sent the original on to the Bishop of Menevia. Perhaps it would be better not to show it to Br Aelred (Carlyle) till we have talked matters over with the bishop. Please keep copy of document for me. It has been changed by the Congregation for Religious, as I did not ask for all as set forth there.

Bishop Mostyn, in a statement which was published in both the Caldey journal *Pax*, and *The Tablet*, stated officially that 'As regards the Abbey itself, the Holy See now recognises it as a canonically established Benedictine monastery with a Novitiate.' Following from all these discussions and consultations, between Bishop Mostyn, Abbot Marmion and the Roman Authorities, a further problem arose, which had to be resolved. This related to the question of lay-brothers in Caldey. In fact, Abbot Aelred had always insisted on a sharing by all the monks in the manual work of the community, and during the Anglican period there were no lay-brothers. All were designated as 'choir-monks,' although Abbot Aelred was the only ordained priest (in Anglican Orders). With the submission to Rome, the community came under the Canon Law of the Catholic Church, which at this time obliged all 'choir-monks' to proceed to the priesthood. It was clear to everyone concerned, that not all the newly converted Caldey monks wished to be ordained priests. The Congregation for Religious agreed to make an exception for Caldey.

Another problem, which Marmion faced in helping the monks of Caldey adapt to their new regime, was in the matter of studies. The previous regime in Caldey allowed little or no time for theological studies as such. The emphasis was on spiritual reading, prayer (public and private) and manual work. The biggest problem for most of the Caldey community was that they knew no Latin. Yet, if they were to become priests, celebrate Mass and administer the sacraments according to the Roman Rite, they would require Latin. Apart from Abbot Aelred, none of the community had studied either philosophy or theology. A solution to this question was provided by Rome, to the effect that Abbot Aelred would be ordained priest after a year's study in Maredsous, but the rest of the community could not proceed to the priesthood without a longer course of studies. It was in connection with this last proviso that the Abbot of Maredsous gave three of his own community to Caldey during the transition period: D. John Chapman, D. Bede Camm and D. Grégoire Fournier. A fourth priest, Father Gregory Stoten, an oblate of Maredsous, completed the formation team.

The new beginning for Caldey, March 1913-Oct 1914
Marmion returned to Maredsous on 17 March 1913, in time for the Holy Week ceremonies, which were early that year. The annalist of Maredsous, in recording the events in Caldey, commented that Marmion was 'full of admiration and thanksgiving towards God, for the wonderful graces that had been given him, in witnessing and taking part in the conversion of the Caldey monks.' Marmion explained to his community that Br Aelred Carlyle (Abbot of Caldey) would spend a year in Maredsous, doing his novitiate and studying theology. The presence of Br Aelred in Maredsous from July 1913 to June 1914 was a constant reminder, not only to Marmion, but to the community of Maredsous, of their involvement in the Caldey Affair.

Marmion had committed himself earlier that year (1913) to travel to Rome and Monte Cassino, in connection with the election of a coadjutor to Abbot Primate Hildebrand de Hemptinne. He decided to take Br Aelred with him on this journey to Italy, which began on 27 April and ended on 8 June 1913. The highlight of the trip was the audience granted to Marmion and Br Aelred by Pope Piux X on 16 May.

It was on this same occasion that Marmion told the pope that he suffered from 'drowsiness, which prevents me from praying,' and received a special blessing from Pius X.

Both Marmion and Br Aelred were back in Caldey by the end of June 1913, to take part in the next stage of the community initiation into Catholic Benedictine life. This was a ceremony to mark the beginning of their novitiate, which took place in Caldey on Sunday 19 June 1913. Bishop Mostyn presided at the Mass which was celebrated by Marmion, during which Br Aelred and his community were given the Benedictine habit. Marmion preached on the text: 'I beseech you, therefore, brethren, by the mercy of God, that you present your bodies as a living sacrifice, holy, pleasing unto God, your reasonable service.' Br Aelred, commenting later on this sermon in a letter, dated 12 July 1913, said:

> The Abbot of Maredsous, Dom Columba Marmion, preached a wonderful sermon to us … After our Communions, we took off our scapulars, and each Brother knelt with it in front of the bishop, who clothed him with it again.

Maredsous becomes more involved, July 1913-July 1914
Br Aelred arrived in Maredsous in mid-July 1913 and remained there – apart from a four months' absence owing to illness – until July 1914. From the very beginning, Marmion and the novice-master (D. Idesbald Ryelandt) decided that Br Aelred should be dispensed from many of the normal rules, and allowed certain privileges. Thus, he was allowed 'a daily walk, generally from 8 to 9 in the morning – an English walk as they call it.' Ordinary novices were forbidden to study philosophy and theology, but in the case of Br Aelred, who was also preparing for priestly ordination, an exception had to be made. All this was in keeping with the injunctions given by the pope to Marmion in relation to Br Aelred. However, it would be wrong to think that Marmion was doing all this without consultation. In fact, he was in constant touch with Bishop Mostyn, who took full responsibility for such points of detail and exemptions. Thus Bishop Mostyn wrote to Marmion on 3 October 1913:

> I am so glad to know that he is progressing not only in spiritualities, but also in philosophy and theology. The sooner he is ready for ordination the more pleased shall I be.

By the end of June 1914, Br Aelred had completed his year's

novitiate and priestly studies. He had evidently given satisfaction to all who were involved in the programme of formation, and was now ready for profession. He made his solemn profession in Maredsous, during a Pontifical Mass celebrated by Marmion, on 29 June 1914. After Vespers that same evening, Marmion convened the Chapter of Maredsous, and spoke of the providential way he and the community of Maredsous had been allowed to help in consolidating the conversions of Caldey.

On 5 July 1914, Br Aelred Carlyle was ordained priest in the abbey church of Maredsous, by Mgr Heylen, Bishop of Namur. The following day he celebrated his first Mass. Marmion, realising that this was a most important moment in the life, not only of Br Aelred, but also of his monks in Caldey, had invited eight of the Caldey community to be present at the profession and ordination ceremonies. On the evening of 6 July 1914, Fr Aelred made a farewell address to the abbot and community of Maredsous, and then set off for his island home on Caldey. He later wrote a more detailed account of his Maredsous experience which was full of praise for all the hospitality and kindness he had received there.

Marmion wished Fr Aelred 'God speed,' as the latter left Maredsous in mid-July 1914, to return to Caldey. They would meet again in Caldey for Fr Aelred's abbatial blessing, on 18 October 1914. By then, the Great War had broken out and Marmion had been forced to accompany his younger monks into exile, first in England and then in Ireland.

CHAPTER 8

The War Years
(1914-1918)

The Impact of the War

The Germans invaded Belgium on 4 August 1914. By 10 August, Marmion realised that the situation was serious, especially as Maredsous was so close to the German border, and might well be in the direct line of the German attack. In fact, the Germans quickly laid siege to the fortresses of Liège and Namur, and captured the latter (only 30 kilometres for Maredsous) on 24 August. By then the monks had opened their doors to crowds of fugitives, both military and civilian, seeking shelter and medical attention. The number of wounded arriving in the monastery every day was so high, that the buildings, normally used to house the pupils of the secondary school and the school of arts and crafts, had to be transformed into hospitals, under the control of the Red Cross. Towards the end of August, Marmion and his monks waited anxiously, while the Germans made their way in the direction of Maredsous, taking village after village. The situation was becoming desperate, with all the monastery's reserve food supplies commandeered to feed the hundreds of extra mouths. The future looked very bleak, indeed, with the threat of possible famine during the approaching winter months.

Always a realist, the Abbot of Maredsous decided to call a meeting of his Council, indicating that he intended transferring some of his community to either England or Ireland during the emergency. He was thinking especially of his younger, student monks, who would hardly be able to continue their studies in Belgium now that war had come. The Council agreed with his proposal, and urged him to go immediately to England to arrange for the reception of his junior monks in that country or in Ireland. It was evident to all that the abbot was the best man for the job. He spoke English and had good contacts among the various Benedictine communities in England. More importantly still, as Ireland was the ultimate destination of the exiled monks, he would be ideally suited for the task of finding a place for them there.

Despite the apparent haste in Marmion's departure from Maredsous, there is no suggestion that he panicked or lost his head. He was certainly not running away, or deserting a sinking ship. His two normal sources of advice, the Abbot Primate (Fidelis von Stotzingen) and Archabbot Schober of Beuron, were both out of reach, the former in Rome and the latter in Germany. He did, however, consult Cardinal Mercier and the Bishop of Namur (Mgr Heylen), who both approved of the idea. It should be noted that he was not the only Belgian religious superior, who took such action at the beginning of the war, a point he emphasised in a letter to Rome, soon after leaving Maredsous:

> In transporting part of the community to England to avoid famine during the approaching winter, I only followed the lead already given by the superiors of various Belgian Benedictine communities belonging to the Subiaco Congregation, Termonde, Steenbrugge, St André, etc. I acted with the sole intention of saving my community, and had no ulterior, political motive in so acting.

Journey to England

Marmion left Maredsous on 8 September 1914, disguised as a cattle dealer and made his way successfully through the war zone to Holland, and thence by boat to England. There are several accounts, written by Marmion himself, giving details of his journey from Maredsous to England. He had to pass through several German army frontier posts, and without passport or papers of any kind, succeeded, not only in getting out of Belgium, but also into England. Soon after landing in England, he went to Caldey Island, from where he wrote to his friend, Fr James Dunne:

> I suppose you have heard that I have just escaped from the Huns (i.e. Germans) with my life. I was surrounded by 30 German soldiers, just on the point of being shot, when Providence intervened. I am looking out for a home for my community, if possible, in Ireland. For the moment I am here giving a Retreat to the Abbot (Aelred Carlyle) and his community in preparation for their profession. Great pressure is

being brought to bear on me from the highest ecclesiastical
and civil authorities, to go to Rome, as the whole current of
Roman opinion is for Germany – against poor Belgium and
England. Our Primate, intimate friend of the Kaiser, is in
great part responsible for that, which makes it very delicate
for me. Pray that God may direct me. I shall be here (Caldey)
till 20th. I dined with Mgr James Ryan of Thurles, in London.

Alone, and with less than 500 Belgian francs in his pocket, he
now faced the formidable task of finding asylum for his monks,
who were due to follow him in batches of seven or eight almost
immediately. Arriving in London, he was approached by some
English friends and asked to undertake a lecture tour on his experiences in war-torn Belgium. However, he resisted this temptation, despite the obvious financial benefits, fearing mainly to
compromise or offend his Beuronese (i.e. German Benedictine)
brethren. Loyalty to the Archabbot of Beuron prevented Marmion
from involving himself in the political or propaganda aspects of
the war. In any case, he had little or no time to waste, as he expected his student monks to arrive at any moment from the con-
tinent. In fact, numbering twenty-three altogether, they left
Maredsous in three groups, on 19, 24 and 25 September. On arrival in England they were given immediate asylum in four
English Benedictine monasteries: Downside, Belmont, Ramsgate
and Caldey.

The Purchase of Edermine House
Obviously such a dispersal of his monks in four different
monasteries could only be considered a temporary expedient. It
was essential to get them under one roof as soon as possible.
Providence stepped in at this juncture to help Marmion solve his
problem. Help came from a most unlikely source, a wealthy
French lady, the Marquise de Bizien du Lézard, originally from
St Brieuc, in Brittany. In reality, this lady was a Benedictine nun,
Mother Marie-Joseph, attached to a convent in the Rue Monsieur,
Paris. She had recently come into a large fortune, and apparently,
the Holy See, through the French Cardinal Billot, had authorised her to use some of the legacy for the purpose of establishing
two Benedictine communities in Ireland, one for monks and the
other for nuns. She had as a companion, Mother Augustine
Savage, of Irish origin, and likewise a member of the Paris community in Rue Monsieur. Both nuns were in England investigating

the possibility of buying suitable properties for two Benedictine foundations in Ireland. Marmion met the Marquise de Bizien in Tyburn Convent, London, early in October 1914, and explained the problem of buying a suitable place for his monks in Ireland. She was delighted at the turn of events, and immediately offered to finance such a purchase, mentioning a sum of 10,000 francs to start him off. This was to be followed by a sum of 50,000 francs, and even more if it was required. She explained her plan in a series of letters, addressed to D. Patrick Nolan (at this time in Ireland looking for a suitable place for Marmion and his monks), and to Marmion himself. She wrote to D. Patrick Nolan on 10 October 1914:

> I regret having missed meeting you when you called recently, as I would have liked to give you my first donation of 10,000 francs for Abbot Marmion. On account of the troubled times, please be good enough to let me know the best way I may send this sum of money to Abbot Marmion. No doubt, Mother Augustine (Savage) will have spoken to you of my wish to make a foundation in Ireland, and at the same time my intention of helping the abbot and monks of Maredsous obtain a suitable place there.

The money was in St Brieuc, Brittany, and it would be necessary for someone to go there, with proper authorisation, to collect it. With this promise of financial backing, Marmion was in a strong position to begin negotiations to buy a suitable property in Ireland. He considered all these negotiations as part of his responsibility as abbot, and he wished personally to see them through to a successful end. It meant a number of visits to Ireland, interviews with the local bishop of Ferns, Co Wexford (Bishop Browne), and meetings with solicitors, etc. He was helped in this task by D. Francis Sweetman, the Downside monk, who was headmaster of Mount St Benedict's, Gorey, Co Wexford. It was Fr Sweetman who introduced Marmion to Bishop Browne and advised him to buy Edermine House, near Enniscorthy, Co Wexford, which belonged to Sir James Power, a wealthy Irish distiller. Fr Sweetman wrote to the Abbot of Downside (D. Cuthbert Butler) on 6 November 1914, saying:

> You may not have heard, in fact you could not have heard, that Abbot Marmion is buying Edermine House for his monks. He is paying £2,000 for Edermine House and about a

hundred acres of land. The price is agreed upon and so we may consider the bargain closed. Abbot Marmion wants the whole matter treated as confidential for the present. He was here (in Mount St Benedict's) last week, and it was I who put him onto Edermine. Considering the way land is going up in this country, he has not done badly. He has guaranteed not to open a school on the lines of ours. The Bishop (Dr Browne) has given all necessary approval.

At this time, there was no question, in the mind of Marmion at least, of a permanent foundation in Edermine. He realised that any such foundation would require a vote by the Chapter of Maredsous, and also the approval of the Archabbot of Beuron. In any case, it was the opinion of most people in November 1914, that the war would soon be over. Marmion probably antic-ipated being absent from Maredsous for only a few months. However, as month succeeded month, and there was no sign of the war ending, he had to reconsider the situation in Edermine. It was his first experience of governing his monks without the benefit of his Council of Seniors. The Seniors and, indeed, the Chapter of Maredsous, were aware of this and looked around for some means of monitoring any developments in Edermine. With this in mind, the Chapter of Maredsous decided, sometime in November 1914, to send D. Aubert Merten, a monk of Maredsous, to help Marmion in Edermine.

Edermine after the arrival of Dom Aubert Merten, Dec 1914-April 1915
D. Aubert Merten arrived in Ireland on 15 December 1914. He had been sent on a dual mission: firstly, to persuade Marmion to return to Maredsous as soon as possible, and secondly, to fore-stall any attempt by Marmion to undertake a permanent found-ation in Ireland. He eventually succeeded in both these matters. By the end of 1914, the regular monastic life had been estab-lished in Edermine, and the twenty or so monks were fully occu-pied in teaching or studying philosophy or theology. There is no doubt that Marmion welcomed the arrival of D. Aubert, and im-mediately appointed him bursar. Throughout the first few months, the finances of the house were rather precarious. Despite the initial promise of financial help given by the Marquise de Bizien, she never endowed Edermine with suffi-cient capital to pay for the day-to-day expenses. Neither had she come up with the large sum of money (50,000 francs) needed to

pay for the actual purchase of Edermine House. Marmion described the dilemma which faced him, coming up to Christmas 1914:

> When I went to present her (the Marquise de Bizien) with the bill for the property (Edermine), she admitted to me that despite her large fortune, she could not come up with the sum in question. All her money, apart from some small amount, was in France, and the bankers were asking 25 per cent to release it, because of all the difficulties with the war in progress … Finding myself faced with this difficulty, I tried to raise a loan, but soon found myself in the hands of a solicitor, who seemed to be determined to rob me of all I had, or at least would not come to any reasonable agreement with me. Thus I had no other choice but to return to the Marquise, and tell her that since no one else was prepared to bring her money out of France, I would go and get it myself. She accepted my offer, and gave me the necessary papers, authorising me to obtain the money.

Marmion left Ireland for Brittany early in February 1915. He arrived safely in France, and went first to Paris, to obtain further papers authorising him to get the money. Marmion then made his way to St Brieuc. After an interview with the Marquise's mother, and having proven his *bona fide*, he was given all the money he required, as well as a box containing the personal fortune of the Marquise, containing several hundred thousand francs. All that remained now was to bring this money safely back to Ireland. By a stroke of good fortune, when passing through the French and British customs, the large box containing the money was not examined, although he himself was subjected to rigid frisking. On arriving back in Ireland, he gave the box and the money to the Marquise, who was obviously relieved at the way things had turned out, and immediately offered him all the money required for the purchase of Edermine.

Thus, by the end of February 1915, Marmion had overcome his major financial worry, the outright purchase of Edermine. From that moment on, he began to make plans for his own return to Maredsous. However, he could not desert his monks in Edermine until he was satisfied that they were capable of managing financially without him. He had already received two letters from his immediate Benedictine superiors, urging him to return to

Maredsous. However much he may have wished to hurry back to Maredsous, he still had many loose ends to tidy up, in regard to the Edermine property.

Above all, Marmion wanted to finalise the relationship between his community in Edermine and the local bishop and clergy. The arrival of D. Aubert Merten gave Marmion more time to attend to this matter. It had already become evident that the monks were having a considerable impact on the local people, who began coming to Mass and confessions to the Benedictine house. They also came for blessings and spiritual help. Marmion realised that the time had come to regularise these spiritual ministrations. On 2 March 1915, Marmion wrote to the Bishop of Ferns, Dr Browne, asking for various favours and permissions:

> On my arrival in your diocese with my band of refugee Belgian monks, Your Lordship received us with open arms and with genuine paternal affection. For this we are, and shall ever be, most deeply grateful. I humbly beg Your Lordship to perpetuate this benevolence by giving us in writing what you so kindly gave us orally on our arrival, the following permissions and favours: (i) Permission to have our abbey church open to the public. (ii) Faculties for the abbot and superior to hear confessions of the faithful, without restriction of time, place or person. (iii) Power to delegate these same faculties to those whom he shall judge capable of worthily exercising them. (iv) Permission for the refugee Benedictine nuns established near us, to have a similar chapel in their monastery. (v) Permission to use in the diocese the various faculties which we have received for blessing medals, crosses, etc, and enroling in the scapular.

The bishop wrote back on 6 March 1915, granting all the permissions and faculties requested. Armed with this letter from the bishop, Marmion was able to approach Fr Murphy, the parish priest of Oylegate and come to an amicable arrangement regarding Sunday Mass in Edermine. Throughout his time in Edermine, Marmion found nothing but kindness and co-operation from the people of the locality. Indeed, he built up such a reputation, that his name has survived to the present day in the folk memory of the people.

The longer Marmion delayed in Ireland, the more he left himself open to the accusation that he was planning a permanent monastic foundation in that country, with himself as superior. The Abbess of Maredret had written to D. Aubert Merten saying that rumours to this effect were circulating in Belgium. Marmion had to dispel such stories and told D. Robert Cornet that 'there is no question of a foundation at this moment in Ireland. Edermine is a simple place of refuge, and nothing more.' There were even some who said that he had become mad, and was 'ill and suffering in the head.' By the beginning of 1916, Marmion had decided that the only way to clear up all the mis-understandings was for him to return to Maredsous.

There was, however, another reason which kept the Abbot of Maredsous from returning to Belgium, namely, his health prob-lems. There are numerous references to this matter in his corre-spondence throughout 1915. Writing to the Abbess of Maredret (D. Cécile de Hemptinne) on 10 June 1915, he told her that 'de-spite my earnest wish to return to Maredsous, the doctors here declare that it would be fatal for me to travel in my present con-dition.' On 8 November 1915, he wrote to D. Robert Cornet, to say that he had undergone a medical examination, and on ac-count of heart trouble, he had been told to rest and put aside all preoccupations. Early in December 1915, he wrote from London, where he had been giving the annual retreat to the clergy of Westminster diocese, to say that he had been ill 'almost to the point of death', and a few weeks later recalled that when, as he thought, he was on the point of death, his greatest pain was to be so far from his Abbey of Maredsous.

On his return to Edermine from London on 19 January 1916, Marmion decided that he should definitely return to Mared-sous. He left Ireland on 8 February 1916 and went immediately to London where he became seriously ill again and had to spend several weeks in hospital. He then went to convalesce with the Benedictine nuns at Ventnor, on the Isle of Wight. On 11 April 1916, he left England for Holland. After one month in Holland, he arrived back in Maredsous on 19 May 1916. He was tired, but happy to be home.

Edermine after Marmion's departure
Even before he left Edermine on 8 February 1916, Marmion had premonitions of trouble among the community he had left behind

in Ireland. He had hinted at this in a letter to the Prior of Maredsous (D. Robert Cornet), on 30 January 1916:

> I have need of your prayers, because some of the young Fathers here in Edermine have pained me by their studied attitude of cold independence towards me ... I try to win them by steadfastness and prayer, but up to now without success.

On the other hand, he did not condemn them, as he told D. Pierre Bastien, his Roman agent:

> They are good, these young monks, but full of confidence in themselves ... They oppose the letter of Canon Law to the spirit of the Holy Rule.

Marmion seems to have failed to appreciate the circumstances in which these young men found themselves. They were, for the most part, still in the process of formation and were going through the unsettling experience of living in exile. They found themselves established in the Irish countryside, where everything was alien: the language, the food, the make-shift way of life. Furthermore, in Edermine they had acquired a new sense of freedom, so different from the rather medieval monastic atmosphere of Maredsous, with its cloisters, enclosure, and above all the example of more than a hundred monks going about their daily round of prayer and other duties. Stability was stamped on every stone of Maredsous. Edermine had no such advantage. It was more like a holiday house than a monastery. And on top of this, there was the continual coming and going of monks, either being called up to serve as *Brancardiers* (stretcher-bearers), in the Belgian army, or returning to Edermine from the war zone for a short holiday. None of the younger monks, that is, those under 25, could hope to escape military service. In many ways, the main concern of those in charge of Edermine should have been that of training the monks for life in the trenches and hospital trains. It was unrealistic to expect them to enthuse about preparing for a future monastic life in Maredsous after the war, when most of them were anxious to serve their country here and now in the war effort. During Marmion's time in Ireland (November 1914-February 1916), the question of war-service only affected the younger monks. But the situation changed radically in 1916, when a new law was passed in Belgium, calling up all those between 25 and 40 years of age. This meant that many of the teaching staff in Edermine were now eligible for military service.

Finally, the political unrest in Ireland, culminating in the Easter
Rebellion of 1916, had its effect upon the little group in Edermine.
The destruction of the General Post Office in Dublin during
Easter week 1916, meant a disruption of the postal service to and
from Ireland. Although the monks tried to live in 'a world apart,'
they were inevitably caught up in the uncertainties of life in
Ireland. This was the time when a new spirit was abroad in the
country, as expressed through the political organisation called
Sinn Féin (Ourselves Alone). Irish freedom and Irish independence were topics of daily discussion not only in public houses,
but in religious houses as well.

The Crisis in Edermine, 1916-1918

The so-called 'Crisis in Edermine' came about through a series
of circumstances, some of which Marmion might have foreseen,
but others were certainly not of his making. That D. Aubert
Merten, the acting superior of Edermine, was one of the main
causes of the trouble, Marmion was the first to admit. In one of
his many letters to the Abbot Primate, dated 12 March 1917, he
said of D. Aubert: 'In my opinion he should be replaced.' But
there was no direct contact between Maredsous and Edermine
during these years (1916-18), which added to the confusion and
misunderstandings. The main circumstance surrounding the
crisis was the uncertain status of Edermine: Was it a fully-fledged
priory (i.e. a monastic foundation as such) or just a temporary
place of refuge? Those monks in the community of Edermine,
who wished to cause trouble, opted to play the monastic foundation card.

Soon after Marmion's departure from Edermine, D. Bonaventure Sodar (Professor of Philosophy) and D. Victor Lejeune
(Professor of Dogmatic Theology) approached the Bishop of Ferns
(Dr Browne), asking him to oppose any move to make a permanent monastic foundation in Edermine. They then made a formal request to D. Aubert Merten (Prior of Edermine), requesting
him to return Edermine to the Marquise de Bizien. They threatened to send a full report to the Congregation for Religious in
Rome if he refused to do as they demanded. D. Aubert was in a
dilemma. He could not accede to their demands, as he was not
one of the trustees or signees of the original contract, drawn up
at the time of the purchase of Edermine. At first he tried to buy
them off, renouncing his title of prior, as apparently this title

implied that Edermine was a canonically erected priory. But this did not satisfy the group of objectors, who insisted that the purchase of Edermine was uncanonical (i.e. against the laws of the church), for two reasons: (a) the Marquise de Bizien, being a religious nun (M. Marie-Joseph), was incapable of making any gift to the Abbot of Maredsous, and (b) Marmion had no right to accept such a gift, since he had not obtained the approval of the Chapter of Maredsous. In order to forestall these objections, D. Aubert Merten decided to write to the Roman agent, who acted on behalf of Maredsous (D. Pierre Bastien), giving him full details of the difficulties he faced in Edermine, and asking his advice. He specifically requested D. Pierre Bastien to contact the Cardinal Prefect of the Congregation for Religious, and obtain a document justifying his (Aubert Merten's) stand on the main issues.

D. Pierre Bastien, instead of telling D. Aubert Merten to forget the whole thing, showed himself rather naïve, and undertook to put the matter before the Congregation for Religious. Both D. Pierre and D. Aubert undoubtedly acted in good faith, but they failed to realise that the problem could have been solved in some other, less complicated, way. In following a particular line of action, they did a great disservice to both the Abbot of Maredsous, and the exiled Belgian monks in Edermine. They set in motion a most unfortunate series of enquiries, visitations and recriminations, which only caused hurt to those concerned.

On 31 August 1916, Cardinal Falconio, the Prefect of the Congregation for Religious, sent the Abbot Primate (Fidelis von Stotzingen) a Rescript on the Edermine affair, asking him to communicate its contents to the Abbot of Maredsous and the monks of Edermine. The Rescript contained two main proposals: (1) that the *status quo* of Edermine remain unchanged until the end of the war, and a decision then to be made by the Chapter of Maredsous, and (2) that silence be maintained on the Edermine question by all parties, under pain of interdict (i.e. penalty). It also contained an admonition to those monks of Edermine who had refused, under pretext of conscience, to obey the regular discipline of the house, and that they should amend their ways. Had everyone acted on the advice given by Cardinal Falconio, the crisis might have been resolved, given time and goodwill on all sides. Unfortunately the affair did not end with the Roman document. On receiving a copy of it, D. Aubert Merten interpreted it as giving him new powers of authority over the community. Indeed, he then made a veritable *volte-face*, and whereas previously he had been happy to renounce the title of prior, he now declared that Rome wished him to resume this title. It appears that the Roman rescript went somewhat to his head, and he began to act with great imprudence. On the other hand, D. Bonaventure Sodar, while accepting the contents of the Rescript relating to the status quo of Edermine, was greatly perplexed to find himself counted among those who were considered as 'disobedient and obstinate.' It seems that D. Bonaventure was under great personal stress at this time, (i.e. the second half of 1916), fearing an early call-up for military service – a fear which was later proved to be unfounded. In order to understand the true situation of Edermine, it is necessary to appreciate the way in which wartime conditions impinged on the issues at stake, causing misunderstandings and misjudgments. Above all, the difficulties of communication between Edermine and Maredsous left Marmion very much at a disadvantage, and prevented him taking any firm action until after the war. It was a heart-breaking experience for the Abbot of Maredsous, who discovered that his beloved Edermine was in danger of falling apart like a house of cards.

The Abbot Primate wrote a long report to Marmion on 4 February 1917, summarising the situation in Edermine as he saw it. Marmion replied to this letter on 12 March 1917, stating that he now regretted having ever appointed D. Aubert Merten as superior in Edermine. For some strange reason, Marmion did not take the obvious step and replace D. Aubert at this stage. If he had done so, most of the ensuing problems could have been avoided. Instead, he proposed another solution, namely, that a Canonical Visitation of Edermine be undertaken at once, preferably by the Abbot of Quarr (D. Delatte) or the Abbot of Farnborough (D. Cabrol). It will not be necessary to go into the complicated details surrounding Abbot Cabrol's two visitations of Edermine. He sent his report of the first visitation to the Congregation for Religious on 8 September 1917. Among the recommendations made by Abbot Cabrol were (1) that Aubert Merten be retained as prior, with D. Lambert Beaudouin as subprior, and (2) that Bonaventure Sodar be sent away from Edermine, to a Benedictine house in England for the duration of the war. Marmion wrote several long letters to the Abbot

Primate over the following months in which he tried to defuse the situation in Edermine. Some of the student monks were eventually sent to English Benedictine houses, while Edermine was put under the control of Abbot Cabrol, as Apostolic Administrator. Throughout all this time, Marmion, who was trying to cope with the deteriorating economic situation in Maredsous, was unable to influence the course of events in Ireland, but was kept in touch by letters from either the Abbot Primate or D. Pierre Bastien. It seemed that most of the crisis in Edermine was over by the summer of 1918, and thus Marmion was able to write to D. Pierre Bastien (in Rome) in a positive vein:

> The news which you give me of D. Aubert and his family (in Edermine), is a great consolation to us all (in Maredsous). It seems that Our Lady clearly wishes to accept the many sufferings and trials through which I have passed, as a necessary means of completing his work … I have, however, a boundless confidence in the paternal goodness of the Heavenly Father, who has never abandoned us.

Marmion seems to have been quite pleased with Abbot Cabrol's arrangements for the running of Edermine. He now hoped that his community in Ireland would survive without any further difficulties, until the end of the war. However, there were still a few difficulties, following Abbot Cabrol's second Visitation (31 July to 3 August 1918). In his report, Cabrol recommended sending all the remaining student monks from Edermine to Quarr Abbey. This was done during the summer of 1918, and again Marmion was quite happy, except for one reservation:

> I regard as providential that our young clerics have been able to retire to Quarr … My only hope is that their stay will not impose on them certain principles and ideas alien to the traditions of our founders, Dom Maur (Wolter) and Dom Placide (Wolter), a sacred heritage which we Beuronese watch over with great fidelity.

Marmion was referring here to differences between the French traditions of monastic life, as they were lived out in Quarr Abbey, and the German-Beuronese monastic traditions of Maredsous. However, before any further steps could be taken, the war ended, with the signing of the Armistice on 11 November 1918. There was great rejoicing all round in both

Maredsous and in Edermine. It was expected that normal monastic life would be resumed in Maredsous, that postal communications would be re-established, the exiled monks return to Belgium, and the future of Edermine decided by a Chapter vote. But, in fact, everything went much slower than expected. Those monks who were in the army, were not released immediately from military service. Postal services took months before being restored to pre-war standards. The exiled monks not in the army, had to get passports and permission to return to Belgium, while the Chapter of Maredsous had so many pressing problems to consider that the question of Edermine could not be dealt with immediately. Marmion himself was absent from Maredsous from 26 December 1918 until 2 June 1919, in France, Switzerland, Italy and Ireland, mainly occupied in business connected with the establishing of a separate Belgian Congregation. Finally, Marmion's health gave him considerable trouble after the war. He spent three weeks in a Dublin hospital (4-23 April 1919), and had to undergo a serious operation. All these facts help to explain the delay in deciding the fate of Edermine and the monks who still remained there after the war ended.

The last days of Edermine, Nov 1918-Feb 1920
There were three things that had to be decided in relation to Edermine, as soon as the war ended: (i) Who was the responsible superior of the house? (ii) Would Edermine continue in existence, as a permanent Irish foundation? and (iii) What was to be done about those monks who had been the main instigators of the Edermine crisis?

D. Aubert Merten was still acting as Prior of Edermine, though Abbot Cabrol exercised certain powers of jurisdiction over the house. Fortunately Marmion was able, within a very short period, to sort this matter out. He wrote to D. Aubert on 23 November 1918, saying that he (Marmion) was now responsible for the affairs of Edermine. Soon after this, he received an official notification from Abbot Cabrol, dated 8 December 1918, abdicating all his powers of jurisdiction over Edermine, and handing back full responsibility to Marmion. In this same letter, D. Cabrol was highly critical of D. Aubert's role as Prior of Edermine:

> If the war had not ended when it did, thus returning the responsibility of Edermine to your hands, I would have withdrawn all authority from the hands of Dom Aubert and put the house under more secure and certain leadership.

Armed with this piece of information, Marmion could hardly
leave D. Aubert in charge for ever in Edermine, and would hardly
appoint him superior of any future Irish monastic foundation.
As regards the possibility of Edermine becoming a permanent
foundation of Maredsous, there were conflicting views expressed by the interested parties. D. Aubert certainly was very
much in favour of a foundation in Ireland, and had even received a young Irish novice into Edermine, as he told Marmion
in a letter, dated 16 November 1918:

> If Edermine becomes, as we all hope it will, a foundation, he
> (the novice) will make profession for Ireland, if not, then for
> Maredsous.

In his letter of 16 November 1918, D. Aubert, after expressing the
hope that Marmion would come to Edermine as soon as possible, paints a glowing picture of life in Edermine – a sympathetic
bishop, and diocesan clergy, local people frequenting the chapel
and coming for blessings, a sound financial basis, good relations
with the neighbouring Irish Dames of Ypres and the Marquise
de Bizien.

Marmion came to Ireland in March 1919, but immediately became very ill, and spent three weeks in hospital in Dublin. While
convalescing in Greystones, Co Wicklow, he heard from D.
Aubert Merten that Dr Codd, Bishop of Ferns, had suddenly
withdrawn all permissions granted by his predecessor, Dr Browne
in 1915, and wished the Benedictines to close the Edermine
house and return to Belgium. Marmion, evidently surprised at
the turn of events, wrote to the Bishop of Ferns asking for an explanation of this sudden dismissal. The reply he received from
the Bishop was short and to the point:

> It was a consolation for us to be in a position to offer asylum
> to the Belgian monks, when calamity befell their country in
> 1914 and they had to flee. We did all we could to make their
> position tolerable during the course of the war. Now, however,
> the end of the war marks the end of their sojourn with us; but
> I quite agree with Your Lordship's suggestion, that a reason-
> able time be allowed for the actual departure.

Evidently the Council of Priests in the diocese of Ferns advised
the bishop on this matter. There were also some complaints
from the parish Priest of Oylegate that a large number of his

parishioners were attending Mass in Edermine on Sundays, with the result that the weekly collection of Oylegate was greatly reduced. But it is also possible that the bishop was influenced by the unfortunate state of affairs in the adjoining Benedictine establishment of Mont St Benedict, in Gorey, Co Wexford. The Superior of Mount St Benedict, Fr Sweetman, had become involved in the political turmoil of the Anglo-Irish war and Bishop Codd was trying to get that place closed as well. D. Aubert told Marmion in a letter, dated 7 September 1919 that 'Dom Sweetman does us a great deal of harm, not only in Wexford, but everywhere.'

By June 1919, Marmion was back in Maredsous, and reported the difficulties over Edermine to his community. Despite all the negative signs regarding a foundation in Ireland immediately after the war, he realised that it would have to be elsewhere than in Edermine. He summarised his ideas on such a foundation in a letter to D. Aubert Merten on 4 July 1919. Soon after this he wrote again to D. Aubert Merten asking the latter to approach the Bishop of Ferns for a extension of their stay in Edermine. However, the bishop refused any moratorium and gave his final ultimatum to the monks on 19 September 1919, saying:

> Your letter has been put before the Council of Priests. They take a serious view of the state of affairs at Edermine, and recommend strongly that the matter should be cleared up at once. The Council states that the departure of the monks from Edermine should, under no circumstances, be delayed beyond one month from the date of this letter.

It was an ultimatum which could not be questioned. D. Aubert, on the advice of Marmion, began immediately to evacuate the remaining monks and to proceed with the auction of Edermine House and its contents. An attempt to get the Marquise de Bizen to take (or buy) back Edermine failed, since her financial position had deteriorated as a result of the war and the devaluation of the French franc. Only two monks remained to organise the rest of the property – D. Aubert Merten and D. Marc de Montpellier. The auction of the furniture, as well as the stock and machinery on the farm, was held on 20 October 1919. The sale of Edermine House could not be held until 27 January 1920. Eventually, the two monks (D. Aubert and D. Marc) left Edermine and moved to a small house which they called 'St Columba's Lodge,' near Macmine (i.e. the convent of the Irish

Benedictine nuns of Ypres), with the permission of the Bishop of Ferns.

Marmion gave a final summing up of the Edermine affair to the Community of Maredsous, on 23 February 1920. He elaborated on the various vicissitudes and difficulties which arose during the years his monks were in Ireland, but pointed out that, in the long run, it had been a successful and worthwhile venture. Maredsous had not suffered financially in any way, but rather had gained to the not inconsiderable sum of 20,000 francs. The principal gain had been the safety and asylum of so many monks during the war. Edermine had been a *pied-à-terre* in a country far removed from the war zone, and Maredsous should be forever thankful to the Marquise de Bizen and the people of Co Wexford, who made it all possible in the first place.

Aftermath
The Official Declaration of the Chapter of Maredsous of 23 February 1920, summarises the positive aspects of the Edermine Affair. It is hard to imagine what Marmion would have done with his younger monks, if he had not taken them to Ireland for the duration of the war. Would their lives have been made any less difficult had they remained in Belgium throughout the war? One cannot say. Most of the monks of Maredsous, who experienced life in Edermine, admitted afterwards that it had been worthwhile. But there was also a negative aspect to the Edermine Affair. Edermine may have served as a safe haven from the Germans, but unfortunately it did not serve as a safe haven from the effects of human weakness and human misunderstandings. It left behind a legacy of suffering and unhappiness in the lives of a few, who had become victims of circumstances not necessarily of their own making.

As soon as the war ended, Marmion began re-organising his monastery, and trying to re-establish life in Maredsous as it had been before 1914. He had first of all to recall those monks who had served in the war, or had gone into exile in Ireland or England. There were twenty monks of Maredsous in Edermine, at one time or other, during the war years.

The war years turned out to be a time of trial for the abbot and monks of Maredsous, but it also bore much fruit. Those who spent some time in Edermine undoubtedly benefitted by the experience, as can be seen by a study of the future careers of some:

D. Bonaventure Sodar and D. Hildebrand Zimmermann founded
the Abbey of Bouveret, in Switzerland, with D. Bonaventure as
abbot; D. Josaphat Ostrowski was the founder of the Priory of
Lubin, in Poland; D. Ildefonse dos Santos Silva went on the mission to Angola, and became Bishop of Silva Ponto; D. Winoc
Mertens and D. Jean-Baptiste Dupiéreux were part of the foundation team of Glenstal Abbey, Ireland; D. Aubert Merten helped
the Irish Dames of Ypres in establishing themselves at Kylemore
Abbey, Connemara, Ireland. 'By their fruits you shall know
them,' can truly be said of the Edermine monks. God had tried
them in many ways, but in the long run, it was an enriching and
a blessed experience for all concerned.

Part III

CHAPTER 9

The Occupation of
Dormition Abbey
(1918-1920)

A week after the signing of the Armistice on 11 November 1918, which brought the First World War to an end, a letter was dispatched from Jerusalem to Marmion. It was written by a military chaplain to the occupying forces in Jerusalem, Dom Dunstan Sibley, a Benedictine monk of Belmont Abbey, England. Wrongly addressed to Abbot Columba at Edermine, Co Wexford, Ireland, it only reached Maredsous on 12 December 1918. It was to set in motion a whole series of activities and negotiations, which occupied the mind and time of the Abbot of Maredsous for nearly two years.

The information in the letter concerned the Benedictine monastery of the Dormition, on Mount Sion, in Jerusalem, which had been in the hands of German monks of the Congregation of Beuron since 1906. The monastery was built on one of the Holy Places in Jerusalem, the site of the Death (Dormition) of Our Lady. It consisted not only of a magnificent church or basilica, but also a monastery and guesthouse. During the 1914-1918 war, the city of Jerusalem was part of the German-Turkish territory, and one of the German monks of the Dormition acted as chaplain in the German army. However, with the capture of Jerusalem by the Allies in December 1917, the position of the German monks in Dormition became difficult. Eventually in November 1918 they were expelled from the monastery and interned in Egypt. What was to become of the monastery? That was exactly what Dom Dunstan Sibley raised in his letter to Abbot Columba Marmion. Furthermore, he had written the letter in a semi-official capacity, referring to the British Foreign Office and the military authorities in Jerusalem.

On receiving this letter, the Abbot of Maredsous discussed the matter of Dormition with his Seniorate on 26 December 1918, emphasising that the exchange of Belgian for German monks in Jerusalem would be received favourably by the British authorities there. The Seniorate gave their general approval to the matter raised by Dom Dunstan Sibley, but recommended that Marmion, who was about to journey to Rome on business connected with a separate Belgian congregation, should take the opportunity of asking the advice of the Abbot Primate and the pope on the Dormition offer. Before leaving Maredsous, Marmion received another letter, this time from Abbot Robert de Kerchove of Mont César, also referring to the Dormition affair. Abbot Robert had heard of this from one of his monks, Dom Lambert Beaudouin, then in Edermine, Ireland, and who had apparently opened and read the letter from Dom Dunstan to Abbot Columba. The important point made by Abbot Robert – at the time President designate of the Belgian congregation – was that he approved of the monks of Maredsous taking temporary possession of the abbey in Jerusalem. This approbation from Abbot Robert undoubtedly gave Abbot Columba some kind of official blessing on the Dormition affair, and led him to believe that the hand of God was in evidence. A second letter, from Abbot Robert, dated 29 December 1918, reached Abbot Columba in Einsiedeln, with further instructions.

Marmion, accompanied by Dom Placide de Meester, left Maredsous on 26 December 1918, barely six weeks after the Armistice. He was undertaking a journey of some five months, which took him to Switzerland, Italy, England and Ireland. This mission was undertaken partly as delegate of Abbot Robert, in connection with the establishing of the new Belgian congregation, and partly on business as Abbot of Maredsous. He faced a daunting task, travelling through post-war Europe, and his health was not too good.

Marmion consults the Abbot Primate and the Pope
On 11 January 1919, Abbot Columba and D. Placide de Meester arrived in Einsiedeln, Switzerland, where the Abbot Primate of the Benedictine Order, Fidelis von Stotzingen, a professed monk of Beuron and a German subject, resided. The primate normally lived in Sant' Anselmo, Rome, but had come to Switzerland during the war to be on neutral ground. Marmion had a number of matters to discuss with the primate, most importantly being the question of the separation of the Belgian monasteries from the

Beuronese congregation. This was a delicate matter, and it required tact and diplomacy on the part of the Abbot of Maredsous not to offend the German-born primate. In fact, the primate was opposed to both the idea of separation and to the Dormition Affair, because both involved an affront to Beuron. We have no detailed account of the conversation between Marmion and the Primate, but in the end the latter was prepared to give way. He agreed that Marmion should go to Rome to consult with the Pope and the relevant authorities there, on the matters of the separation and Dormition. For some strange reason, the primate gave no hint at this stage to Marmion that a decision had already been made in Rome by the Sacred Congregation for Religious, to send Italian monks of Subiaco to Jerusalem to replace the expelled German monks in Dormition. This oversight on the part of the primate was to cause some difficulty and embarrassment to the Abbot of Maredsous when he arrived in Rome. What is quite clear from the correspondence of Marmion is that he left Einsiedeln for Rome believing he had at least the tacit consent of the Abbot Primate to proceed with the Dormition and the separation affairs.

Marmion arrived in Rome on 21 January 1919, to discover that the monks of Subiaco had already been charged by Cardinal Gasparri, the Papal Secretary of State, to take possession of Dormition. Everything had been arranged through Mgr Serafini, the Secretary of the Congregation for Religious, who had formerly been Abbot President of the Cassinese Congregation. However, the British authorities in Jerusalem had not been consulted, and all the arrangements had been made through Abbot Raphael Molitor, of St Joseph's Abbey, Westphalia, Germany.

Notwithstanding this apparent *fait accompli*, Marmion decided to put the matter before Pope Benedict XV, during an audience he was granted on 26 January 1919. According to his own account, contained in a letter to D. Gerard François, the Prior of Maredsous, dated 28 January 1919, he made a strong protest regarding the sending of Italian monks to Jerusalem. At the end of this interview, the pope decided to overrule the existing arrangements, and to commit the mission to the monks of Maredsous. This seems an almost unbelievable turn of events, but all the evidence shows that this is what happened. Marmion was ordered by the pope to inform Mgr Serafini of the change of plan, and also to see Cardinal Gasparri on the same matter. Both Serafini and Gasparri were understandably surprised at the decision of the pope.

The Abbot of Maredsous went first to see Mgr Serafini, a fellow Benedictine. Evidently the latter was so impressed by the direct order of the pope that he acquiesced immediately, and cancelled the arrangements already made to send the Italian Cassinese monks to Jerusalem. However, the interview with Cardinal Gasparri was not so easy. It took all the persuasive powers of Marmion to convince Gasparri to consent to the change of plan, thus clearing the way for the Abbot of Maredsous to send his monks to Dormition. He only won this concession at a price. Cardinal Gasparri, an astute diplomat, demanded a written guarantee or promise, from Marmion, to the effect that the latter:

> ... undertook to restore the monks of Beuron to the monastery of Dormition, as soon as circumstances permitted them to retake possession.

In other words, Cardinal Gasparri made it clear to the Abbot of Maredsous that he considered the Dormition occupation by the Belgian monks to be temporary. It was to be nothing more than a holding operation. Time alone would show how long this holding operation might last, but for the moment the ground had been cleared for Marmion to take action.

Negotiations leading up to the departure for Jerusalem
On 30 January 1919, Marmion sent a telegram to the Prior of Maredsous, saying that the 'Pope wishes to send four monks immediately to Dormition.' The following day, Abbot Marmion named one of these four, D. Grégoire Fournier, as superior of the newly constituted Dormition community. He also ordered that D. Grégoire, with his three companions (D. Emmanuel Valet, D. Fueillen Mercenier and D. Hugues Delogne), were to leave Maredsous as soon as possible and proceed to Paris, where they would meet Marmion on 27 February, and receive their final instructions.

The Abbot of Maredsous left Rome on 15 February, 1919, and was in Paris on 27 February to meet his four monks who had been designated for the Dormition foundation. He gave them their final instructions, as well as official letters to the religious authorities in Jerusalem. The four Maredsous monks finally embarked from Marseilles on 4 March 1919, and arrived in Jerusalem on 11 March. They were to remain there until 1 November 1920.

Marmion faces further difficulties

During the first three weeks of March 1919, Marmion was travelling through England, visiting some of his monks who were installed in Farnborough and Quarr Abbeys, and also attending to various commitments in two Benedictine convents, Tyburn and Ventnor. He then crossed over to Ireland, and reached Edermine on 20 March, where he was due to begin a canonical Visitation. On arriving at Edermine, he found a long letter awaiting him from the Abbot Primate, dated 22 February 1919. After referring to the separation of the Belgian Abbeys from Beuron, and confirming that neither he nor Mgr Serafini, the Secretary of the Congregation for Religious, would offer any obstacle to the proposed breakaway, the Abbot Primate then turned to the question of Dormition. He expressed his surprise at the decision of the pope, cancelling the arrangements to send the Italian monks to Jerusalem, and permitting the Belgian monks to take their place. He also complained that Abbot Raphael Molitor of St Joseph's Abbey, Westphalia, had not been consulted by the Roman authorities over the change of plan.

The Abbot of Maredsous wrote in reply from Edermine Priory on 21 March 1919, expressing his surprise that any misunderstanding could have occurred. This letter is very important as it explains the way in which such misunderstandings could have arisen. Marmion recalled his interview with the primate in Einsiedeln, when no mention was made of the negotiations between Abbot Raphael Molitor and the Italian monks. Realising the delicate situation, the Abbot of Maredsous reiterated his intention of restoring Dormition to the German monks, if and when circumstances allowed.

The primate replied on 29 March, repeating that he was extremely upset by the turn of events regarding Dormition Abbey. At the same time he exonerated Marmion from the suggestion that the latter had deliberately deceived the pope. However, the affair had been an embarrassment to the primate, and he did not know how he could satisfy the injured party, i.e. Abbot Raphael Molitor. He claims that he thought he had explained his point of view clearly to Marmion, in their original meeting in Einsiedeln. It was only on receipt of the letter from Marmion, dated 7 February 1919, that he, the primate, discovered this was not so.

Marmion had no doubt in his own mind that the pope and Cardinal Gasparri had given their full consent to the Belgian monks going to Jerusalem. He received a confirmation of this in a letter, dated 21 March 1919, from the Count de Salis, the British Ambassador in Rome, who declared that:

> On 31 January, Cardinal Gasparri had asked me to issue visas for the four monks of Maredsous, in place of the four Italian monks.

Early in April, Marmion received a welcome word of encouragement from Cardinal Gasquet, who was writing to acknowledge the copy of *Christ in his Mysteries* which the Abbot of Maredsous had sent him:

> Now as to the Dormition matter, I don't think I should let it bother you at all. I do not suppose that you will hear anything more. It is quite clear to me that nothing was said about Abbot Molitor having arranged for the Subiaco (Italian) people to go to Jerusalem. Had it been known, I am certain that the English government would have refused to permit the Italians to go, when they were acting with the Germans. For this reason, it is a very good thing that they were not allowed to go in the end.

Marmion takes stock of the situation

While in Ireland, Marmion had time to reflect on the various problems and misunderstandings surrounding the Belgian takeover of Dormition. He was, above all, anxious to exonerate himself *vis-à-vis* Abbot Raphael Molitor. This latter, who believed that he was still responsible for the Abbey of Dormition, wrote twice to the Abbot of Maredsous, explaining his point of view. A close scrutiny of these letters leads one to believe that Abbot Molitor overlooked three important factors:

1. The difficulty of communicating between Germany and Rome, Ireland and Switzerland during the post-war months.

2. The fact that Germany had been defeated in the war, and there was a widespread anti-German feeling throughout France, Belgium and England. The Belgians had suffered very great material damage during the war, and they wished to exact reparations from Germany by way of compensation. There was even the possibility that Dormition Abbey could be considered as part of this overall reparation payment, made to the Belgians by the Germans.

3. The question of financial support for Dormition could no longer be entrusted to the original Deutsche Verein of Cologne, seeing the collapse of the German currency. Abbot Molitor was thus in no position himself to maintain Dormition Abbey, either from the personnel or financial point of view. Someone had to step in to fill the gap, and the monks of Maredsous were prepared to do this, with the blessing and approval of the pope and the Sacred Congregation for Religious.

While convalescing after an illness in Dublin, at the end of April 1919, Marmion decided to put on paper his views relating to the Dormition Affair. Whether this was intended as an *aide mémoire*, or just a copy of an official document to be sent to the Abbot Primate or Abbot Molitor, it is impossible to say. However, his views were given in reaction to the publicity given in the Belgian national press on the Dormition Affair. One such article, entitled 'Nos Bénédictins à Jérusalem,' appeared in a newspaper *Vers l'Avenir* on 1 March 1919. At no time did Marmion enter into communication with any Belgian newspaper, and one wonders, therefore, where the newspapers got their information. His apparent 'reflections' of April 1919, were merely an expression of his anxiety over the Dormition mission. He realised his personal responsibility for the monks he had sent to Jerusalem. His thoughts, at this time, went with them, and he constantly prayed that his monks would be able to face up to the challenge he had set them.

Abbot Marmion appeals to Belgian and British governments
However, time was running out, with the Paris Peace Conference due to complete its work by the end of the year. If any influence was to be exerted on the delegates in Paris, to ensure that Dormition Abbey remained in Belgian hands, then it had to be done quickly. Marmion now decided to play the patriotic card: declaring that Dormition was a little piece of Belgium – in fact the only Belgian property in the Holy Land. It had to be retained and maintained, with the help of the Belgian government. On 12 June 1919, Marmion wrote to M. Léon Delacroix, the Belgian Foreign Minister, asking him to take up the Dormition Affair with the Belgian delegates in Paris. At the same time he had a circular letter printed, seeking financial help for the Dormition monastery. This circular letter was addressed to 'some generous Belgians, in support of work which was essentially religious and patriotic.'

Marmion continued his efforts to gain support for the Maredsous occupation of Dormition. This time he approached the Belgian government, through the Minister for Foreign Affairs, M. Paul Hymans. The latter in turn asked the Belgian Ambassador to the Holy See, the Comte Léon d'Ursel, to raise the matter with Cardinal Gasparri. The reply of Cardinal Gasparri to the Belgian Ambassador is a diplomatic 'tour de force'. The Cardinal held out no hopes to the monks of Maredsous that they would ever be given permanent possession of Dormition. He insisted that they were simply 'caretakers' or guardians, until such time as the German (Beuronese) monks could return to Jerusalem. The same message was relayed to D. Grégoire Fournier by D. Placide de Meester, who had a private audience with Benedict XV on 1 September 1919: They must await the decision of the Paris Peace Conference; while the occupation of Dormition by the Belgian monks may be prolonged, it could hardly be a permanent arrangement.

The Abbot of Maredsous was grateful for the sums of money which were already coming in for Dormition, donated by well-wishing Belgians, and promises had been made of annual subscriptions, ranging from 5,000 to 100 Belgian francs. On 21 December 1919, Marmion wrote to D. Grégoire Fournier to say that:

> The subscriptions for Dormition are very numerous. We have on hands 40,000 francs in outright gifts, to which must be added 20,000 francs of annual subscriptions. If we have to leave Dormition and hand over the property to the Germans, it may be possible to settle elsewhere in Palestine. The Belgian government would very likely help us in such a case.

In fact, the Belgian government did come up with financial help. Marmion acknowledged this in a letter dated 5 April 1920, addressed to M. Hymans, the Foreign Minister. However, despite these last minute efforts made by the Belgian Foreign Minister to influence the Paris Peace Conference in favour of the Maredsous monks retaining Dormition, there were other forces working towards the restoration of the German monks to Jerusalem. On 2 June 1920, Abbot Raphael Molitor wrote to the Abbot of Maredsous, thanking him 'most profoundly for the great service which the monks of Maredsous had rendered in Dormition.'

The last days of the Belgian occupation of Dormition
On 2 August 1920, D. Grégoire Fournier learnt from Sir Herbert Samuel, the British High Commissioner in Palestine, that 'all the Germans who were expelled could now return,' save a few named persons. That same day he received official notice in writing:

> With reference to your conversation this morning with the High Commissioner, His Excellency desires me to inform you that Peace having been signed with the German government, all German nationals who have applied for passports in the ordinary way will be allowed to return to Palestine. Every effort will be made to notify you in advance in the event of the German Benedictine Fathers returning to your convent.

D. Grégoire wrote at once to the Abbot of Maredsous, informing him that the expelled German monks could now return to Palestine, and asking for instructions. He gave his considered views on the line of action which might be taken, under four headings:

> 1. We will return Dormition to the Germans on their arrival.
> 2. No attempt should be made to initiate any other foundation in Palestine by the monks of Maredsous.
> 3. The Germans should be asked to return to Jerusalem as soon as possible, to avoid further expenses to the Belgians.
> 4. Asks that he, D. Grégoire, would be informed as soon as it is known when the Germans will return, so that the Belgian monks may withdraw with dignity.

On 14 August 1920, a further dispatch reached D. Grégoire from General Sir Ronald Stors, the Military Governor of Jerusalem, stating: 'I have the honour to inform you that the Latin Patriarch of Jerusalem has received permission for the return of the German Benedictine Fathers to the Dormition Convent.' For his part, the Abbot of Maredsous, as soon as he received official notice of the return of the German monks to Jerusalem, wrote to Cardinal Gasparri, saying that he was withdrawing the Belgian monks immediately, and arranging for every facility to be given to the Germans to reoccupy the Abbey of Dormition. At the same time, Marmion wrote to the Belgian Foreign Minister, notifying him of the changed situation in Jerusalem and stating that he was recalling the four Maredsous monks from Dormition

Abbey. He concluded by thanking M. Hymans for his financial help and encouragement in recent months.

One cannot but be struck by the way the Abbot of Maredsous decided so quickly to wind up the Dormition Affair, without any apparent regret or recrimination. From all the evidence, it seems quite clear that he had at no time held out any firm hope of a permanent presence of his monks in Palestine. The fact that the question of a foundation in Jerusalem was never discussed in the Chapter of Maredsous is proof of the tenuous situation all through 1919-20 in the mind of Marmion.

All that remained now was to make an orderly withdrawal from Jerusalem, before the arrival of the German monks. On 19 August 1920, the Abbot of Maredsous called a meeting of his Council, asking their advice on what steps should be taken in relation to the changed situation in Jerusalem. Finally, on 22 August he wrote to D. Grégoire Fournier, outlining the procedures to be adopted:

1. An immediate departure of all the Maredsous monks from Dormition;
2. No question of any other foundation – at least for the moment – in Palestine;
3. D. Grégoire to take a holiday, visiting the Holy Places for a month, but the other three monks return to Maredsous as soon as possible;
4. D. Grégoire had full authority to use his discretion in winding up the financial affairs and putting the Dormition property in proper order, in view of the return of the German monks.

Marmion concluded with a very sincere thanks to D. Grégoire and his three companions for their wonderful work in Jerusalem, done under obedience.

On receiving these instructions, D. Grégoire set about making the necessary arrangements. On 8 September 1920, he wrote to the Abbot of Maredsous that he would hand over the keys of Dormition Abbey to the Latin Patriarch, and not await the arrival of the German monks. However, he pointed out that it would take some time to tidy up and pack their effects, not to mention two retreats which had to be preached. He concluded rather optimistically, that 'All four monks would leave by boat for Marseilles by 22 October 1920.' In fact, it was on 1 November 1920 that D. Grégoire wrote the final section of his diary: 'All Saints Day. At 7.30 Abbé Cretan photographed the group. At 8.30 departure of three Fathers in two cars. May God protect them. End of the Community of the Dormition.'

However, the last words on the Dormition saga must be left to two German Benedictines, who were personally connected with the Jerusalem house, both before and after the Belgian tenancy. On 3 October 1920, Abbot Raphael Molitor wrote to Marmion thanking the latter for his letter announcing the withdrawal of the Belgian monks from Dormition. He pointed out that it would take some weeks to arrange the replacement of the Belgian by the German monks, and ended with the following genuine words of thanks: 'I would like to renew my thanks to your Fathers for their faithful work.' This tribute, by the President of the Beuronese congregation, proves that the earlier misunderstandings were now all forgotten, and that the German abbots recognised the important role which the Abbot of Maredsous and his four monks had played, in preserving Dormition Abbey during the very difficult post-war years.

The second German Benedictine, whose judgement on the Dormition Affair must be taken as of considerable import, was D. Maurice Gisler, who had been superior of Dormition before the war. He wrote to D. Grégoire Fournier on 24 October 1920, almost, one might say, with tears in his eyes:

> The 13 years which we (i.e. the German monks) spent in Jerusalem, were not free from difficulties; but ours were nothing compared to those which you had to encounter, in a situation so new and so uncertain. It is this fact which urges me to thank you sincerely and in the name of us all, for all your devoted work in the Holy Sanctuary which was so sacred to us ... We do not know as yet who will be your successors as Guards of Honour in the Basilica of Our Lady of Mont Sion (Dormition). But it is our duty to thank you for having continued with so much dignity what we began ... Our thanks especially to your Abbot Columba for making such an excellent choice of his personal deputy. Our thanks to you, and to Rev Father Emmanuel and your two confrères, for the spirit of sacrifice and good zeal which you have shown in this work of peace ... May the Queen of Heaven

recompense your good and holy services, and in recognition of your stay in her Sanctuary in Jerusalem, may she grant a long and prosperous era to the venerable Abbey to which you are returning.

Thus ended the temporary occupation of the Abbey of Dormition by the monks of Maredsous. They had proved themselves trustworthy 'Guards of Honour' in this sacred shrine to Our Lady of Mount Sion. Throughout the whole affair, Marmion had proved himself a tactful and loyal son of St Benedict. His actions were completely vindicated by the subsequent history of Dormition. The 'holding operation' which he initiated saved the abbey from possible extinction. As far as he was concerned, the affair was over, and both he and his monks had emerged with honour.

CHAPTER 10

Formation of the
Belgian Congregation
(1911-1922)

It was inevitable that the violation of Belgian neutrality by the Germans in 1914, followed by the destruction of so many cities, towns and property, would lead to a wave of anti-German feeling in that country. Maredsous was within the German occupied zone, and the monks had to witness the day-to-day spectacle of German soldiers and army vehicles on the roads and countryside. The words 'collaborator' and 'collaboration' were already in common use, bringing disdain and retribution to those guilty of helping the Germans. By force of circumstance as well, of course, as for patriotic reasons, the monks of Maredsous had to distance themselves from any contact with the Germans. The Abbot of Maredsous had already made clear his attitude towards the Germans when addressing his community in June 1916, in the aftermath of the visit of Kaiser William II to his monastery. Long before the end of the war, it had become obvious to most people that Maredsous would have to cut its links with the Beuronese (German) congregation, to which it had belonged since the foundation of the abbey in 1872.

However, Maredsous was not the only Belgian Benedictine abbey to be so affected. Mont César, in Louvain, also formed part of the Beuronese congregation. What was to be done? Would these two abbeys set up a new congregation, or would they affiliate to some other already existing congregation? Normally, the Roman authorities would require at least three abbeys to form a congregation, and thus there existed a dilemma or obstacle which would have to be overcome. The Abbot of Maredsous (Marmion) and the Abbot of Mont César (Robert de Kerchove) met and decided, first of all, to take all necessary steps to break with Beuron and, secondly, to establish a Belgian congregation. The process would undoubtedly be a lengthy and complicated one, involving communication with Rome, with the

Abbot Primate (Fidelis von Stotzingen) and the Abbot President of the Beuronese congregation (Raphael Molitor). The burden of most of the negotiations was to fall on the shoulders of Marmion, as the Abbot of Mont César (Robert de Kerchove) pleaded age and poor health as an excuse for not being directly involved.

Facing up to the German question
Marmion found himself having to make a very difficult personal decision in breaking away from Beuron. His own monastic roots were deeply set in Beuronese traditions. Maredsous had been founded by Beuron, and most of its everyday customs and usages had been imported from Germany. On top of this, Marmion was by nature a traditionalist. Having lived for more than thirty years under a particular regime, he was not so anxious for any radical change. Certainly, the move towards separation from Beuron did not come from any social reasons on the part of the Abbot of Maredsous. He approached the affair with all the objectivity he could muster, in a strictly business-like manner. The separation affair gave him an opportunity to prove his ability in difficult negotiations, and definitely disproves the suggestion that Marmion was a poor administrator.

Already in 1910, there had been some talk of Maredsous breaking away from the Beuronese congregation. At the time, D. Jules Jonckheere, Subprior of Maredsous, had suggested that all the Belgian Benedictine houses (Maredsous, Mont César, Afflighem, Steenbrugge, Termonde, etc.) should unite in a kind of national congregation. However, at the time (1910) Marmion disagreed with the proposal for separation, and wrote to the Archabbot of Beuron, Ildefonse Schober, on 9th February 1910:

> I am entirely opposed to such a project. I hold fast to the Beuronese congregation with all the fibres of my heart, and I shall never consent to be separated from it.

However, early in 1915 he had changed his mind, influenced no doubt by his own wartime experiences. Writing from the comparative peace of the Irish countryside on 11 November 1915, he had written to Archabbot Schober:

> After having prayed and reflected very much, I am persuaded that, no matter what the final result of the present struggle may be, the dependence of the Benedictine houses in Belgium and England on the Archabbey of Beuron would be

prejudicial and impossible. The good of our houses in Belgium and England makes it imperative that we devise, without delay, the means of effecting this separation, while at the same time remaining united in heart and in spirit.

Marmion left Ireland on 8 February 1916 and, after a long delay due to a serious illness in London as well as the difficulties in getting the necessary visas to travel to Belgium, eventually arrived back in Maredsous on 19 May 1916. He soon realised the difficulties of living in German-occupied Belgium. Several of his monks were in prison in Germany, but there were many other reasons to make him succumb to the general anti-German mood of the Belgian people. He wished under no circumstances to compromise himself. The first major test of his patriotism came when Kaiser William II visited Maredsous on 23 June 1916. Marmion decided, without hesitation, not to be present in Maredsous when the Kaiser arrived, but spent the afternoon with the Benedictine Sisters of Maredret. He took the same step to absent himself from Maredsous when the German Governor of the Province of Namur visited the abbey in that same month of June 1916. One particular order given by the Germans annoyed Marmion very much. This was in connection with the daily time-table, which had to be regulated according to German time, not Belgian time, and had been forcefully introduced in November 1915, before the return of Marmion to Belgium. It was a daily reminder to the monks that they lived under German rule.

The situation of the two Belgian abbeys in the last months of the war
Sometime towards the end of the war, the Abbot of Maredsous caused to be drawn up a Memorandum, which was entitled 'A confidential note on the situation of the Belgian Benedictine abbeys.' Although neither signed nor dated, it is possible from internal evidence to date it after June 1916, and the style is clearly that of Marmion. It deals with the question of a 'Separation from Beuron,' under three headings: (1) the Facts, (2) the Consequences and (3) the Remedies.

1. *The Facts:* The two Belgian abbots have to act under the authority of a German superior. This dependence entails constant exchange of letters and visits between the German and Belgian abbeys. One of the most objectional results of this mutual contact is the appearance in the Belgian abbeys of visiting German monks, some of whom are fighting in the

German army. The Germans have used the Belgian abbeys for propaganda purposes, and even hoped that the German Emperor would have been received solemnly in Maredsous.

2. *The Consequences:* There is a danger that those Belgian monks who are fighting for the Belgian flag will feel betrayed by their confrères in the monastery, whom they see as fraternising with the enemy. The German bishops and clergy (including German Benedictine monks) have continually supported the action of German soldiers in Belgium, whereas the Belgian bishops (and especially Cardinal Mercier) have condemned the German occupation of their country. Resulting from this, the Belgian hierarchy have broken off relations with the German hierarchy. The Belgian Benedictines should follow this lead, and break off relations with the Beuronese congregation.

3. *The Remedy:* It is only the Holy See that can bring an end to the dependence of the two Belgian abbeys on the congregation of Beuron. The Papal Nuncio in Brussels should act as an intermediary between Rome and the Belgian Benedictine abbeys situated in the German-occupied part of their country. It may be necessary to use other diplomatic sources, such as the Belgian Ambassador in Rome, to deal directly with the Cardinal Secretary of State. For the moment, i.e. until the end of the war, the two Belgian abbeys should be placed directly under the Holy See.

The first steps towards separation

On 20 December 1918, Marmion went to Mont César, to confer with Abbot Robert de Kerchove on the question of separation from the Beuronese congregation. They agreed to take the necessary steps towards forming a separate Belgian congregation. The Abbot of Maredsous was invited to put his ideas before the Seniorate of Mont César, and was able to tell them that the Seniorate of Maredsous had already given their unanimous consent to the creation of a new, independent congregation. At the end of this session, the Abbot of Mont César said that he was prepared to accept the proposals made by Marmion, and obtained the unanimous support of his Council. From all the evidence available, it seems clear that the Abbot of Maredsous was the prime mover in the whole affair, and it was thanks to his energy and determination that the separation question got off the ground.

On 23 December 1918, Marmion called a meeting of the Chapter of Maredsous to discuss and vote on the separation issue and the setting up of a Belgian congregation. The Annals of Maredsous give the following account of this meeting:

An important meeting of the Chapter, to discuss the separation – which has become a matter of necessity – of our Belgian abbeys from the congregation of Beuron. Father Abbot is proposing to go to Rome to treat of this matter with the Holy Father, after first taking the advice of the Abbot Primate, who is at present residing in Einsiedeln.

The Acts of the Chapter of Maredsous give a more detailed account of this meeting on 23 December 1918, and refer to the efforts of D. Jean de Hemptinne to set up a Belgian missionary congregation. The Chapter accepted the fact that the two abbeys of Maredsous and Mont César would constitute a very small group to start a new congregation. It was suggested that Edermine Priory (in Ireland) and Erdington Abbey (in England) be asked to join, to form a more composite group. At the end of the Chapter meeting, a vote was taken on three issues or proposals. The vote was unanimous in favour of:
1. Separation from Beuron.
2. Fr Abbot Columba and D. Placide de Meester going to see the Abbot Primate and the pope.
3. The setting up of a new congregation, consisting of Maredsous and Mont César to begin with.

Soon after this, the Abbots of Maredsous and Mont César got together to draw up an address to Pope Benedict XV, dated 29 December 1918. It was planned to show this address first of all to the Abbot Primate for his approval, and then to present it to the pope. It is a very clear statement of the case for separation, stressing the antipathy felt by the Belgian people towards the Germans because of the sufferings endured during the war. The two abbots also stated that the Belgian government would not tolerate any contact between Belgian nationals and Germany. Under the circumstances, it would be impossible for Maredsous and Mont César to remain under Beuronese rule.

Marmion, accompanied by D. Placide de Meester, set out for Switzerland on 26 December 1918. The former was full of enthusiasm and good spirits, despite the time of the year and the difficulties of travelling across frontiers only six weeks after the ending of the war. They reached Paris on 1 January 1919, hoping to get all the necessary papers for entering Switzerland from the French and Swiss authorities.

Despite all their visas and papers, the two travellers were held up for several days at the Swiss frontier. In fact, D. Placide was arrested and kept in prison for forty-eight hours and questioned by the French police. They later discovered the reason for this inconvenience, namely, the fact that they were going to see the Abbot Primate, who was a German citizen. On arrival in Einsiedeln on 11 January 1919, they were told that:

> This place, in the opinion of the Swiss and French police, is a nest of Bosches (i.e. German) spies, who were being entertained by the Abbot Primate.

There was another reason for the police becoming suspicious of the two Belgian monks: D. Placide was carrying some gold coins and was accused of trying to smuggle them into Switzerland. It was hardly an encouraging start to their mission, but it prepared them for the many other hurdles they would have to take in the months ahead.

The Abbot Primate gives his reluctant approval
Despite their rather discouraging experiences en route to Switzerland, once Marmion and D. Placide reached Einsiedeln, they were able to relax and feel at home. Indeed, D. Placide paid a genuine tribute to the hospitality they received both from the Abbot of Einsiedeln (D. Thomas Bossart) and the Abbot Primate (Fidelis von Stotzingen). They needed to be at their ease if they were to succeed in their double mission: to consult with the Abbot Primate about Dormition Abbey in Jerusalem and to get his approval for the separation of the two Belgian abbeys from the Beuronese congregation. All through these early negotiations in Einsiedeln, one comes to realise that there is one important element missing, i.e. a representative of the Abbot President of the Beuronese congregation. But given the post-war circumstances, and the anti-German feelings at the time, it would be difficult for the Belgian monks to sit down at the same table as a German abbot. It is true that the Abbot Primate was also German, but his office was international. Abbot Robert of Mont César recognised this, as he intimated to the Abbess of Maredret

in a letter dated 23 Jan. 1919, explaining why Marmion had been sent to Einsiedeln in the first place. The idea was to get the primate's support, so that their case might be better received in Rome. A few days later he wrote again to the Abbess of Maredret, saying:

> I am so happy that Abbot Columba was able to meet the Primate before going on to Rome. It would have been so difficult to act without him.

Considering all the preliminary discussions which had gone on in reference to the separation of the Belgian monasteries from the Beuronese congregation, one can hardly believe that the Abbot Primate knew nothing of the matter when Marmion broached the question of separation. We have several accounts of the actual meeting of the two abbots in Einsiedeln. The overall atmosphere seems to have been cordial, according to the account given by the Abbot Primate to the Abbess of Maredret:

> Abbot Columba's stay in Einsiedeln was perfect. He remained from 11-16 January, and we understood each other well. I had already read *Christ, The Life of the Soul* and was delighted with it. As for the separation, I saw immediately that the matter was already decided and that there was no way to change things. I regret it very much and I consider it an unfortunate step both for our monasteries and the entire Order. But, I admit, that given the present (political) situation and the imperfection of men – it is inevitable.

At the end of their discussions, the two abbots, having weighted all the arguments carefully, decided:

1. To accept the principle of separation.
2. For the present, the new congregation would consist of only two abbeys, Maredsous and Mont César.
3. Notice of the proposed separation should be sent to the Abbot President of the Beuronese congregation (D. Raphael Molitor).
4. That the Abbot of Maredsous should go to Rome to submit the proposal of separation to the Sacred Congregation of Religious.

Marmion consults the Roman authorities
Abbot Columba and D. Placide de Meester arrived in Rome on 21 January 1919. On 26 January Marmion was received in audi-

ence by Benedict XV, and immediately got down to the business of discussing the separation of the two Belgian abbeys from the Beuronese congregation. The Abbot of Maredsous had brought with him the address to the pope, drawn up by himself and the Abbot of Mont César before he had left Belgium, and which the Abbot Primate had endorsed with his signature on 15 Jan 1919. According to the account given by Marmion to D. Gérard François, dated 28 Jan 1919:

> The Holy Father was charming and kept me twenty minutes. He understood the situation perfectly, and told me he would himself undertake to send our supplication to Mgr Serafini, the Secretary of the S. C. of Religious (which, indeed, he did) and that there would be no difficulty.

On the face of it, this seems like an exaggeration but in fact, the original copy of the supplication, now kept in the archives of the S. C. of Religious in Rome, is clearly endorsed, in the pope's handwriting, with the words: 'This request seems to merit to be received favourably. B. XV.' It was as strong a recommendation as anyone could wish for, and helped to have the matter dealt with expeditiously and satisfactorily by the S. C. of Religious.

Marmion was received graciously by the Prefect of the S. C. of Religious, Cardinal Scapinelli, who told him that 'there would be no difficulty about breaking away from Beuron.' However, Mgr Serafini, the Secretary of the S. C. of Religious, pointed out that 'the setting up of the new Belgian congregation would take time and that it would have to pass before a full session of cardinals.' On 5 February 1919, a letter from Cardinal Scapinelli, addressed to Marmion, confirmed the official agreement of the Holy See to the separation of Maredsous and Mont César from the Beuronese congregation. Thus the first stage of the negotiations had been successfully completed. Until the second stage was completed, i.e. the setting up of the Belgian congregation, the two abbeys were to be directly under the Holy See.

St André provides a third abbey for the Belgian congregation
Owing to his various journeys to England (for the visitation of Erdington Abbey) and to Ireland (for the visitation of Edermine), as well as being very ill in a Dublin hospital for most of the month of April 1919, Marmion was unable to give his full attention to the separation issue, until his return to Maredsous on 2

June 1919. He had been absent from his monastery for more than five months. One of the first matters to occupy his attention, was the possibility of inviting the Abbey of St André, in Bruges, to join in with Maredsous and Mont César, to form the new Belgian congregation. There were many good reasons for taking this step, not least being the fact that in order to establish a new Benedictine congregation, it would be necessary to have a minimum of three monasteries. There was no question of inviting the three abbeys belonging to the Subiaco Congregation of the Primate Observance (Afflighem, Steenbrugee and Termonde), as they had very different traditions and customs from those of Maredsous and Mont César. The Abbey of St André, however, had been founded by a monk of Maredsous, D. Gérard van Caloen, in 1899, and though its main work was missionary, it had many links with Maredsous.

This matter was discussed at a meeting of the Abbot's Council or Seniorate in Maredsous, on 5 June 1919. According to the minutes of this meeting:

> Father Abbot Columba read out an official letter from Abbot Théodore Nève, proposing the union of St André with Mont César and Maredsous, to form a Belgian congregation.

On 6 August 1919, the Chapter of Maredsous met in full session to vote on the question of admitting the Abbey of St André into the future Belgian congregation. By a large majority (33 to 7), the Chapter agreed to the motion, having been given guarantees that St André would take responsibility for its debts and its mission to Katanga. On 16 September, D. Laurence Zeller, the Apostolic Administrator of the Brazilian congregation, authorised the Abbey of St André to separate from its commitment in Brazil, and to join the Belgian congregation.

The formation of the Belgian congregation
Throughout the latter months of 1919, the three abbots of Maredsous, Mont César and St André met frequently to discuss a new constitution for the Belgian congregation. They set up a commission, which was chaired by Marmion, with two delegates from each of the abbeys. D. Célestin Golenvaux and D. Ursmer Berlière were the delegates from Maredsous. By January 1920, considerable progress had been made and a draft outline of the constitutions sent to Rome for approval.

On 20 February 1920, by the Apostolic Letter, *Ordo a divo Benedicto*, Pope Benedict XV set his seal on the erection of the new congregation. It was to consist of three monasteries of monks: Maredsous, Mont César and St André, which were to form a new congregation under the title of the Annunciation. At the same time, two decrees of the Sacred Congregation of Religious, both dated 7 February 1920, laid down the norms of the new congregation, concerning such matters as the constitutions and the position of the abbot president. Until such time as the first Chapter General of the new congregation met, Abbot Robert of Mont César would exercise all the functions of president.

The Aftermath

Marmion, always sensitive to the feelings of others, and wishing to soften the sufferings of the archabbot over the separation issue, wrote to Beuron on 20 April 1920:

> I am so sorry to hear that my letters have not reached you. I wrote a letter full of sincere affection from the bottom of my heart, and I was surprised not to have received any reply ... I now repeat what I have already written, that from the bottom of my heart I remain even more attached to Beuron, to its spirit and traditions, than before the war. If I have had to take any active part in the steps leading to the separation, that was simply on account of pressure from the government, at the request of Abbot Robert and of my community. The government has been very strict: some communities, which have not taken the steps we have taken, have had their goods confiscated and have suffered in different ways. This separation is for us a great loss in every way, because at present we are reduced to a very small congregation, which will find it hard, at least in the beginning, to maintain itself.

Archabbot Walzer replied to this last letter on 29 April 1920, in terms which showed that any past bitterness or misunderstanding had by now been forgotten:

> There has never been any doubt in my own mind, or that of my community, of the basic need for separation. I rejoice that the Belgian abbeys have now been given the right to develop and to run their own affairs. A powerful tree does not suffer any essential damage if you cut a large branch from it.

Floreat, crescat! (May it flourish and grow). On the 18 of this month, I read to my community the Apostolic Brief of Benedict XV. The only words which I added to the text (of the Papal Letter) were a thanksgiving for all the affection which we have received from you in the past, and the hope of continued fraternal relations in the future.

A final postscript must be added to this story of the separation. On 15 October 1922, the Abbey of Maredsous celebrated its Golden Jubilee of fifty years of its existence. It was a magnificent occasion, at which Marmion presided. There was only one cloud overshadowing the event: no German abbot or monk was either invited or present. Although four years had passed since the end of the war, patriotic feelings still ran high in Belgium. The Abbot of Maredsous would dearly have liked to invite the Abbots of Beuron and Maria Laach, but it was politically impossible.

Yet, as always, he tried his best to soften the hurt which this exclusion might have caused his German confrères. Beuron had been very much involved in all the events the monks of Maredsous were now celebrating. Without Beuron there would have been no Maredsous. He thus decided to write to Archabbot Walzer to explain the situation. It was not an easy letter to write, but both charity and justice demanded that he do so. He chose his words carefully:

> At the moment, when we are preparing to celebrate, with great joy and thankfulness, the Jubilee of 50 years since the foundation of Maredsous, a cloud overshadows our hearts. This cloud is in the absence of yourself and the other abbots of the dear Beuronese congregation. We owe everything to our Mother Beuron. It would have been for us all, and especially for the elders among us, a great and profound joy to receive you here, and to see you among us on that day. For myself – and God is my witness – it has been a great sorrow not to be able to invite you, because I love Beuron, and venerate the memory of its founders Maur and Placide (Wolter), who are our founders also. May I ask you, my dear Father Archabbot, to unite with us in prayer and thanksgiving to God, for all that he has done for us through our dear founders.

Marmion had the courtesy to dispatch this letter more than a month before the date of the Jubilee, to show his sincerity and the solidarity he continued to feel towards Beuron, despite the separation and the continuing political uncertainties. In his heart of hearts, he would dearly have loved to dispel this one cloud, which overshadowed the Jubilee celebrations, but it was just not possible.

CHAPTER 11

The Last Years
(1920-1923)

There is no doubt that the physical and psychological suffering which Marmion had to undergo during the war years undermined his energy and health. This is very clear from many of his letters, especially those written throughout 1922. Writing to his niece, Mother Scholastica Joyce, on 6 July 1922, he said:

> If I were to follow my own inclination, I would give my resignation as abbot, and retire for my last years as chaplain to a convent, to pray, write, and rest while preparing for the last voyage.

Early in August 1922, he met an old and dear friend, Madeleine Bodart, who lived near Maredsous. She was shocked by his appearance and said to him: 'How you have changed! You seem so tired,' and he had replied, 'Pray for me, I have become old, and I don't expect to live long.'

During these last years he suffered from overweight and was often found to fall asleep when sitting in a chair, even in his choir-stall.

Yet, during the final years, Marmion never reduced his work load. In addition to a very heavy correspondence which he attended to faithfully, he continued to give regular conferences to the community in Maredsous, and to preach retreats in Belgium, France, England and Ireland. A random check in his 'diary' for 1920 shows that he preached to the seminarians of St Edmund's College, Ware, England (9-3 August), while in 1921, he gave the retreat to the clergy of Westminster (1-6 August) and the Poor Clare Colettines in Cork, Ireland (5-14 November). But what took up so much of his time during the years 1919-21 was the work involved in establishing the Belgian congregation and drawing up the new constitutions. This latter work involved meetings in Mont César, Louvain, with Abbot Robert de

Kerchove as well as in Maredsous, with Marmion presiding. It was Marmion who had conducted all the negotiations – in Einsiedeln and Rome – leading up to the separation of the Belgian monasteries from Beuron. He now had to undertake the tedious task of preparing all the legal documents for the newly formed Belgian congregation.

There was, however, one consolation – one might even call it success – which came his way during these last years. He had become, almost overnight, a best-selling author, with the publication of his spiritual trilogy: *Christ, The Life of the Soul* (1917), *Christ in His Mysteries* (1919), and *Christ, The Life of the Monk* (1922). They were eventually to be translated into thirteen languages. The Abbot of Maredsous received almost universal acclamation and congratulations. Pope Benedict XV wrote a personal letter to him, and later told the Abbot of Maredsous that he used *Christ, The Life of the Soul* as his spiritual reading. It would be impossible to give a summary of all the eulogies passed on the books of Marmion. It was a great test of his humility to be told that he was considered a master of the ascetic life, and that his books were spiritual classics. There is no evidence that all this adulation went to his head. He was as much surprised as others by the success of his books. However, it did mean that during the last years of his life he became a well-known and well-loved international figure in Catholic circles. His writings brought honour to his monastery, and henceforth the two names, Maredsous and Marmion, became almost synonymous.

The changing face of post-war monasticism
Marmion reached his sixtieth birthday on 1 April 1918. By then he had become set in his ways of thinking and acting. He was very much the product of his age – the so-called Victorian Age. The upheaval in European society which came about as a result of the First World War, seemed to be a betrayal of all the values he had ever held dear. The post-war years presented him with a challenge as he tried to understand the strange ways of his younger monks. He realised that new beginnings had to be made, after the long years of war, during which many of his monks had been absent from Maredsous. His involvement in setting up the new Belgian congregation brought home to him the fact that monasticism itself was facing a challenge in the post-war world. It would require a great deal of tact and patience to cope with the demands of the New Age.

He admitted all this in a letter to his friend, Mother Berchmans Durrant. After quoting St Benedict on the role of abbot (or superior), he paraphrased this task as 'governing souls and becoming the servant of the characters and whims of many ... Let us help each other by our union with Jesus. My Cross at present is very heavy ... I am beginning to feel the effects of my age.' He was, above all, beginning to feel the effects of the New Age which emerged from World War One. This New Age brought a revolution in society, votes for women, the breaking down of barriers, an independence of spirit, and so on. The war had turned the world outside the monastery upside down. It would gradually turn the world inside the monastery upside down also. Many of his monks, who had served in the war, had faced death many times as *brancardiers* (stretcher-bearers) or chaplains. They knew how to obey orders, but they had also learned to interpret an order. Their army experience helped them to grow up, to mature, to think for themselves. For the most part, they had come from close-knit Catholic families and had very little experience of the world before entering the monastery. Suddenly they found themselves thrown into the world of the trenches, with its stark reality of rough language and rough living. They could not shake off all these experiences at once on returning to the cloister. Many had left Maredsous at the beginning of the war as mere children; they returned to Maredsous in 1918 as adults. It was not going to be easy to adapt, to get back into the regular life of the monastery.

What they really needed was a kind of 'half-way house', somewhere they could have time to adjust, before they were asked to settle down to monastic life. For many, it was too sudden a change from the trenches to the cloister. Neither the Abbot of Maredsous, nor any other religious superior at the time, thought of such a thing as a 'half-way house.' The amazing thing is that so many did eventually adjust to monastic life, and went on to become excellent monks. Perhaps the most serious challenge facing the younger monks who had served in the war was getting back to their priestly studies, which they had interrupted in order to serve their country. This called for some hard adjustment and much self-discipline. At this time, all choir-monks were expected to go on for the priesthood. Indeed, most of the young *brancardiers* had been ordained subdeacon or deacon, although they had not yet begun their theological studies. Finally, and perhaps most important of all, these young soldiers had fought for their country and some had been wounded. They were heroes, and expected to be treated as such. All they got was an army pension and special travel facilities on Belgian railways. It was something of a let-down.

Marmion was certainly filled with some apprehension at the thought of the arrival in Maredsous of these young ex-soldiers, many of whom had been with him in Ireland at the beginning of the war. As early as 23 November 1918, he had expressed his feelings to D. Aubert Merten, Prior of Edermine:

> I am rather fearing the arrival of these young monks, who have for so long been deprived of our traditions and our monastic spirit.

Above all, he feared that they might form themselves into separate groups or 'cliques,' and thus disturb the unity and peace of the monastery. His fears were not unfounded, at least in the case of a minority (seven or eight). At the same time, it must be said that the majority of those who had served in the army returned to Maredsous and settled in to monastic life without too much trouble to themselves or to their abbot. It was in trying to cope with the minority, i.e. those who had difficulty in settling in, that the Abbot of Maredsous had to suffer much heart-break and trouble, especially during the years 1920-1921.

Pilgrimage to Lourdes, 18-26 September 1922
Marmion visited Lourdes only once in his lifetime, a few months before he died. It was a memorable experience for him, having had a life-long devotion to Our Lady. During his days in Clonliffe, he had always signed his name 'Joseph A. Marmion, E. de M (Enfant de Marie).' As he grew in age and spiritual maturity, he formulated his own ideas into a theological synthesis:

> Mary is above all else, the Mother of Jesus, whose mission it is to form us in her image.

He selected Rosary Sunday for receiving his abbatial blessing in 1909, and commemorated this event each year with a procession in honour of Our Lady of the Rosary.

In September 1922, Mgr Heylen, the Bishop of Namur, asked Marmion to lead the annual diocesan pilgrimage to Lourdes. Although Marmion had already undertaken a great number of external activities that summer, he felt this was an opportunity he could not miss. The Abbot of Maredsous set out by train from Namur on 18 September, with over 2,000 pilgrims, many of them invalids. He shared the spiritual duties of hearing confessions, saying Mass, helping the sick, reciting numerous rosaries and other prayers, as they passed through Belgium and France.

While in Lourdes, the Abbot of Maredsous sang a Pontifical High Mass in front of the Grotto. During his homily he said:

> My heart is overjoyed to see this great witness of filial love of her children towards Mary.

He was evidently much moved by his stay in Lourdes and he expressed his feelings in a letter to a young Irish nun:

> Just got back from Lourdes, full of love for Mary.

He had brought two of the Maredsous monks with him – D. Eucher and D. Izard – as well as his sister, Mrs Joyce. This pilgrimage to Lourdes was one of his last public appearances, although he could not have known it at the time. It brought joy to his heart and helped to keep up his morale during the final months of his life. On his return to Maredsous, he immediately gave his attention to the forthcoming Golden Jubilee of his monastery, which had been founded on 15th October 1872. This Jubilee was to be his swan song.

The Golden Jubilee of Maredsous, 15 October 1922
The Abbot of Maredsous called a meeting of his Council on 16 January 1922 to make arrangements for celebrating fifty years of Benedictine life in Maredsous. It was decided that it would be a religious festival, and invitations were to be sent to Cardinal Mercier, Mgr Heylen (Bishop of Namur), all the Belgian Benedictine abbots, the Provincials of religious orders, the local clergy, local civil dignitaries, and other important lay people. It was also decided to publish an illustrated booklet, giving the history of the past 50 years, and to strike a commemorative medal. A committee was appointed to coordinate all the arrangements. At the same time, a group of lay people – Friends of Maredsous – decided to mark the occasion by presenting a new bell to the abbey church.

One may well ask if it was really necessary to have this Golden Jubilee celebration. Was it not a form of ecclesiastical triumpalism, quite out of keeping with the post-war austerity, still felt in many parts of Europe? The Seniors of the Maredsous Council were well aware of this problem, but decided that 'the social position of the monastery, and its relations with the ecclesiastical and civil world, called for such a celebration.' It would be an occasion for thanking all those people who had been associated with the abbey at one time or another since its foundation in 1872. Marmion also felt that the Jubilee would help to unite his community. They would have to show a united front and make a common effort to guarantee its success. One gets the impression, however, after reading all the evidence, that the matter was really taken out of the hands of the Abbot of Maredsous once the original decision had been taken. According to the annalist, D. Raphaèl Proost, there was a very strong pro-Jubilee lobby in the community. Writing some time after the event, D. Raphaèl criticised some of the newspapers for concentrating on the external side of the celebrations, i.e. the history of the abbey, the beauty of the countryside, the splendid liturgical ceremonies, 'without touching the real internal and family side of the celebration, or the personality of Abbot Columba.'

As far as the Abbot of Maredsous was concerned, the Jubilee represented a family occasion, when he and his monks could be 'at home' to all their friends and well-wishers. But it was even more than this; it was an occasion to thank God for all the graces and blessings bestowed upon Maredsous and its monks over the past fifty years. It was, finally, the first occasion for Maredsous to show its face to the world since the formation of the Belgian congregation. Marmion wanted everyone to know that nothing had been radically changed and that they still cherished the memories and traditions of their Beuronese founders, Abbots Maur and Placide Wolter. In the commemorative marble plaque, erected in the monastery cloister at the time of the Jubilee, the names of the first two Abbots of Maredsous were written in large, coloured letters. The only cloud that hovered over the Jubilee celebrations was the absence of any German abbots. The political situation at this time (1922) was too tense to allow either the Archabbot of Beuron or the Abbot Primate, to attend.

Sunday, 15 October, turned out to be a fine day, with sunshine and blue skies. Cardinal Mercier presided at the pontifical High Mass, which began at 10.30 am. Abbot Robert de Kerchove, the

President of the Belgian congregation, and many other Benedict-
ine abbots, attending along with Mgr Heylen, the Bishop of
Namur. A special place of honour was reserved for Madame
Henri Desclée, the only surviving signatee of the original Act of
Foundation in 1872. The sermon was preached by M. l'Abbé
Crépin, the Dean of Fosse.

After the Mass, there was a banquet in the abbey school for the
monks and their guests. There were numerous speeches, among
which that of M. Joseph Desclée was perhaps the most moving:

> In inviting me to speak here today, it was clearly the inten-
> tion of the organisers to pay their respects to my family, who
> have been called the founders of the abbey. However, we
> only founded the body (i.e. the buildings) of the abbey. It is
> the monks who have provided its soul and spirit, and over
> the past fifty years have sanctified these stones.

The Golden Jubilee of Maredsous turned out to be the last public
appearance of Abbot Columba. A few weeks later, he went to
Paris to preach a retreat to the Benedictine sisters of Rue
Monsieur. It was to be his last retreat. By the end of December
1922, he was suffering from an attack of influenza, which soon
developed into something more serious. He wrote to D. Placide
de Meester on 29 December: 'Pray for me. I feel very old.' The
end was nearer than anyone, including himself, thought at the
time. Within a month of writing to D. Placide, he was dead.

The last journey of Abbot Columba
Abbot Columba gave his last conference to the nuns of the abbey
of Maredret on Sunday, 17 December 1922. He had intended
giving them the annual retreat, but had to withdraw because of
illness. However, he felt well enough to give the final lecture,
and it is interesting to see how he dwelt on the theme of 'Death':
'For some time past, each morning, at Mass, I have asked Our
Lord to give all those who die the grace to be assumed into his
death. If we are faithful in making this prayer to Our Lord, we
can be assured that, at the moment of our own agony and death,
Jesus will do for us what we have so often asked for others.'

The Annals of Maredsous under the date 31 December 1922,
refer to the custom of the community during the end of the year
reunion, of drawing a patron saint for the New Year. Abbot
Columba drew St John of God as his patron, and remarked to
some of the brethren that he would be needing an infirmarian

(or nurse) in the near future. Belgium experienced a serious 'flu epidemic' throughout December 1922 and January 1923. Abbot Columba was one of those who was struck down with the flu just after Christmas. He had not completely recovered when he went to Brussels and Malines to fulfil a number of obligations. He travelled by motor car and became quite ill while in Brussels. On returning to Maredsous on 5 January, he seemed to rally somewhat, and thought himself well enough to spend a week in Antwerp, where he had his portrait painted.

He returned to Maredsous on Saturday 20 January, and the following day gave the usual Sunday conference to his monks. He told them how much he had been struck, while in Antwerp, by the painting of 'Christ in Agony' by De Luripias. On Monday 22 January, he held a Chapter meeting, and some of the monks remarked how unwell he looked. However, he made no complaints and continued his rounds of prayer and work. On Wednesday 24 January, he appeared in the refectory wearing his 'caban,' and said that he felt cold. The following day he was unable to celebrate Mass, though he did receive Holy Communion. He told his prior, D. Célestin Golenvaux: 'I am all the time thinking of death. Hardly an hour passes by without my thinking of death.' He felt well enough to celebrate Mass the following day, 25 January, having promised a nun friend in Virton that he would offer Mass for her deceased mother. He had also promised a very dear Irish nun, who had joined the English Convent in Bruges, and was due to make her profession on 25 January, that he would offer Mass for her that day. In fact, one of his last letters was written to this nun, Sister M. Fidelis Tidmarsh, on 23 January 1923, in which he said: 'I have very deep sufferings of heart and soul at present; I know you pray for me, as I do daily for you.' Right up to the end, however, he was thinking of his many friends, especially his spiritual daughters, and he felt close to them in his hours of suffering.

During this last weekend of his life, Abbot Columba seemed to be asleep for most of the time. He had moments of lucidity, and replied to some of the questions put to him, but at no time initiated any conversation. He said 'Thank you' for any services offered him during these last days, but never asked for anything. He showed great patience and courage, and seemed to have abandoned himself into the hands of those who were nursing him, as well as into the hands of God. When one of his monks said to him: 'Father Abbot, are you happy to go to heaven?' his reply was simply, 'the Will of God.' At other times, to this same question, he replied, 'Very happy, yes, very happy.'

Abbot President Robert de Kerchove of Mont César came to visit Marmion on Monday 29 January, and stayed up to the end. D. Raymond Thibaut was also present at the bedside of the dying Abbot of Maredsous, and asked Marmion for a blessing. However, the latter was unable to raise his hand, and said simply, 'Bless me, please,' which D. Raymond did.

Soon after 6.30 pm on Tuesday 30 January 1923, Abbot Columba began his last agony, and said suddenly to D. Eucher Foccroule,'Help me, help me!' The Abbot President led the prayers for the dying, followed by the recitation of the Rosary. For the next three hours, prayers were recited until 9.30 pm when a sudden change was noticed. Marmion breathed his last at 10 pm, while those around him recited the 'De Profundis' and the 'Subvenite' and other prayers. The next morning, the body was brought to one of the monastery parlours and laid out for the veneration of the hundreds of clergy and people, who came to pay their last respects.

The funeral took place in the abbey church of Maredsous on Saturday 3 February, with Pontifical Requiem Mass sung by Mgr Heylen, the Bishop of Namur. Cardinal Mercier had hoped to perform the last rites of his friend but was prevented from doing so by illness. Abbot Columba was laid to rest in the monastery cemetery, under the shadow of the abbey church.

CHAPTER 12

Marmion as Abbot

Dom Marmion was Abbot of Maredsous for a little over 13 years, from 28 September 1909 to 30 January 1923. He was 51 years of age at the time of his election and at the height of his powers, both intellectual and physical. Although he had never previously exercised full authority in a monastery, he had some experience of ruling over others, especially during his ten years as Prior of Mont César in Louvain. It appeared to many that his whole life up to his election as abbot was a preparation for ruling over the community of Maredsous. His election came as no surprise, either to himself or to others. He had built up a reputation as a man of God and a man of prayer, as well as being an eminent retreat-giver and wise confessor. If one were to pinpoint a single factor which influenced those who elected him as abbot, it was his reputation for preaching sound doctrine. This was borne out during the pre-election retreat which Marmion gave in Maredsous in September 1909. The community recognised that they had in Marmion a man who was a master of the spiritual life, and capable of providing them with a spiritual leadership. Owing to the enforced half-yearly absences from Maredsous of his predecessor, Abbot Hildebrand de Hemptinne, the monks were starved of doctrinal guidance. Marmion would surely provide them with solid and sound spiritual teaching. At this time, abbots were elected for life, so the monks of Maredsous were fully aware that he could be their superior for the next twenty years or more.

Marmion on the role of the abbot
There is no such thing as a perfect abbot. Marmion had enough humility to realise that he was far from perfect. He had to face a very considerable challenge, being all things to over one hundred monks, day after day. However, he prayed that God and his monks would overlook his faults and not let these be a hindrance

to the salvation of the souls committed to his care. Despite all his cares, anxieties and ill-health, he maintained an inner calm, thanks to a constant union with God through prayer. He had an unshakeable faith in God, and was a complete optimist in dealing with souls.

He was convinced that as abbot he held the place of Christ in his monastery. But this was not a license to practise tyranny, rather that he had to act as a father to all. On his appointment as Abbot of Maredsous, he had taken as his motto: To serve rather than to be served. He was determined to be at the service of his monks, and to maintain peace and charity at all costs. The Roman Censor, appointed to study his writings, stated that he could find no evidence of Marmion ever violating this rule of charity, and that this charity was 'constant, unalterable, generous to the point of forgetting himself to an uncommon degree'.

In Chapter 3 of his book, *Christ, the Ideal of the Monk*, Marmion has written at length on the role of the abbot in the monastery. The programme which he outlines for the abbot is not a theoretical, but a practical and realistic one. Marmion considers that the first duty of the abbot is to act as pastor. He sees this pastoral responsibility as a caring one, which calls for kindness and gentleness. But it implies, above all, the responsibility to teach wise doctrine. The abbot must be in close touch with God, and should strive to contemplate in prayer the divine law brought by Christ, in order to be a beacon-light of truth to others. It is quite evident from the context of his reflections, that Marmion is writing from his own experience.

The norms of Marmion's government

First of all, Marmion based his government on the Rule of St Benedict. He knew the text by heart, and was able to conjure up phrases and ideas from the rule to suit every occasion, especially when he commented on the rule during his weekly conferences to his monks. Many of these conferences were taken down verbatim by his monks, and later formed the basis for one of his books, *Christ, the Ideal of the Monk*. Marmion had meditated on the rule for more than twenty years before becoming abbot. He had first of all put St Benedict's various injunctions into practice in his own life, before proposing it to others. Above all, he was convinced that the rule was 'a simple and very safe guide for leading to God'. It had brought him, personally, to a close union with God, and he wished to encourage his monks to follow this same sure path of the rule.

Secondly, Marmion insisted on a close following of the Beuronese constitutions – at least up to the establishment of the Belgian congregation – which he considered to be the most authentic interpretation of the Rule of St Benedict. On 11 November 1915, he told Archabbot Schober that the Beuronese constitutions were 'the best adaptation of the Rule of St Benedict' and that nothing could diminish his affection and attachment to the spirit of Beuron. There was nothing *avant-garde* about Marmion. On the contrary, he showed himself to be a traditionalist, in that he treasured old and tried spiritual values.

Thirdly, Marmion believed that his monks should obey the laws of the church, (i.e. Canon Law and Liturgical Ritual). He had a profound respect for the magisterium of the church, and kept in close touch with the Roman authorities. When the New Code of Canon Law appeared in 1917, Marmion gave his full submission to all its injunctions. One particular injunction, which was given a more detailed treatment in the Roman Decree *Quem ad modum*, forbad superiors and novice-masters to hear the confessions of their subjects. Marmion did not hesitate to promulgate the decree immediately, even though this matter had caused him some personal problems during his time in Edermine. Ever since his days as a student in Rome (1879-1881) he maintained a great respect for the person of the pope. As Abbot of Maredsous, he was received no less than five times in private audience by a pope.

Marmion as leader and initiator
When Marmion was elected Abbot of Maredsous in 1909, he had approximately 130 monks. Within a few years, in 1913, this number had increased to 144. That year (1913) there was 78 professed monks, plus 6 novices and 6 postulants for the choir, and 50 brothers (*conversi*) plus 1 novice-brother and 3 postulants-brothers. In 1914 the community had increased to 148 monks in all. After the war, owing to the German brothers having to leave Belgium for political reasons, the community in 1921 was reduced to 126. Of these 92 were choir-monks and 34 *conversi*. Marmion certainly maintained the numbers in his monastery throughout his time as abbot, and saw a very considerable increase in the number of choir-monks. According to the *Liber*

Scrutiniorum of Maredsous, Marmion received 65 choir-monks and 8 *conversi* into the monastery between May 1912 and October 1922. Another source for information on numbers is the Book of Professions. From this latter book one can see how Marmion was occupied each year, clothing novices, holding simple and solemn professions, administering minor orders, etc. Apart from the war years, 1914-1916, he attended to these matters himself.

As Abbot of Maredsous, Marmion was determined to give a lead especially in liturgical matters. He saw his monastery as a centre of prayer, not only for himself and his monks, but for a much wider clientele. Pope Pius X gave a great impetus to liturgical studies by his decree on frequent communion. Marmion took up the challenge. He attended a liturgical week in Louvain in July 1911, and gave three of the main conferences. In these conferences he makes what was then an original suggestion, that the laity as well as the clergy have much to gain by living the liturgical year.

Marmion made history in 1912, when he hosted a liturgical week from 19-24 August, in Maredsous. He gave an inspiring opening speech, in which he refers to the liturgical movement several times. He also gave the opening conference on *Le symbolisme dans les Deux Testaments*. In many ways he shows himself a pioneer in his approach to both liturgical and scriptural studies. His words were an inspiration to his audience, which included many of his monks.

However, it was not only in the spiritual, but also in the temporal domain that Marmion gave a lead. He was, it seems, a firm realist in practical matters, and liked to get things done well and in proper order. Thus it was during his regime that electric light and central heating were installed in the large monastic buildings, and the monastery was also equipped with modern baths. The abbot had plans for a new building to house the rich monastery library, but they had to be abandoned when the 1914 war broke out. He would not have considered himself a financial expert, but he insisted that the monastery remain out of debt, and that the income exceeded the total annual expenses.

One very important financial matter had to be settled by Marmion after the war, namely, the title and legal ownership of the monastery property by the abbot and the community of Maredsous. Apparently, a religious house could be considered a charitable trust by the newly voted (1921) Belgian law A.S.B.L. But when the monastery was founded in 1872, no legal title was given to the monks by the Desclée family. Such a gentleman's arrangement could no longer be upheld. It was a delicate matter and Marmion had to exercise very considerable diplomatic skill in finding a solution. He was helped in all this by D. Gérard François, his chief financial advisor. The matter was also discussed in the Seniorate, but the final decision rested with the abbot and M. Benoît Desclée. The difficulties and misunderstanding were evened out, and the legal documents completed by October 1922, before the Golden Jubilee of the foundation of Maredsous. It was a matter which had haunted Marmion since the beginning of his abbacy. Throughout the lengthy negotiations he retained the friendship and affection of the Desclée family.

Marmion and the abbey schools
The monks of Maredsous had two schools to maintain: the *Ecole Abbatiale,* a secondary school, which had been established in the very early days of the monastery, and the *Ecole de Métiers d'Art,* (Arts School), which was established in 1903 during the abbacy of D. Hildebrand de Hemptinne.

Marmion was determined to keep the two schools going, and took a personal interest in the details of running them. He encouraged his monks who were engaged in this school work, believing that it gave them a chance to live out the vow of stability within the cloister. Although he had not himself been a success, as either a class-teacher or *surveillant,* (House-Master) in the *Ecole Abbatiale,* he had always retained an interest in the school and in its pupils, especially the past pupils.

Now, as abbot, he decided that he had to be a father to the pupils of both schools, just as he was to his monks. The pupils lived under his roof, and formed part of the monastic *familia.* He wanted the pupils of both schools to feel at home in Maredsous. One of his favourite phrases for the monastery was *moutier,* which means in English a monastic home. He had the facility to adapt to young people to tell them stories and make them laugh. The pupils were the first to notice the difference between the pomp and ceremony of the very few visits made to the school by Abbot Hildebrand de Hemptinne, and the frequent visits of Abbot Marmion.

Personal contacts with his monks

Marmion kept in close touch with his monks, first of all by regularly inviting them, one by one, to his room for a monthly interview. It was customary, at this time, for monks to present themselves once a month before their abbot, for a private or spiritual tête-à-tête. During such an interview, the monk would normally give an account of how he spent his time, what was the state of his health and spiritual life, and in return, received from his abbot whatever directives or instructions were necessary to help him progress in his monastic life. Marmion saw his job as that of encouraging his monks to greater efforts, in their spiritual and secular pursuits.

He also kept in touch with his monks by letter. Out of the 1,700 letters of Marmion which have survived, 257 were written to the Priors of Maredsous, while 181 were written to one or other of his monks. Undoubtedly there were many others, which have been lost. In these letters, Marmion shows a remarkable ability to understand the difficulties of his monks. In general he adopted an open and affectionate approach, as of a father to his children. He also had a special charism in winning the affection and friendship of the families of his monks. Over and over again, he writes how he felt at home in the family circles of his monks. He adopted a warm relationship with most of the parents of his monks, stayed at their houses, and created a very important bond between their families and the monastery.

Marmion had a very talented community. Many were internationally renowned servants or artists. There is no evidence that he was ever jealous of their success or honours. He believed that by their work and public recognition, they brought honour to Maredsous. The *Revue Liturgique et Bénédictine*, in 1913, gave a lengthy eulogy on D. Ursmer Berlière, on his appointment to the post of *Conservateur en chef de la Bibliothèque Royale* in Brussels. There was an element of Belgian patriotism attached to the acceptance of such a post, and it could be called 'serving King and country'. Marmion gave his full approval and put no obstacle in the way of D. Ursmer Berlière.

Marmion believed in allowing his monks to develop their natural talents, no matter where they had to work, provided they were giving these services for God. One such monk was the artist, D. Adelbert Gresnigt. When Marmion became abbot, D. Adelbert was already engaged on a major work in the crypt of the abbey of Monte Cassino. It was not completed until 1913, when there was a solemn opening, which Marmion attended.

On completion of this work in Monte Cassino, D. Adelbert was then invited to work on the painting of a Benedictine Abbey Church in Sao Paolo, Brazil, on a two years contract, with Marmion's permission. The war broke out and he obviously could not return to Maredsous. He wrote to Marmion in 1915 asking for instructions. According to the Memoirs of D. Adelbert, Marmion, who received his letter during the Edermine interlude, asked D. Adelbert to remain in Sao Paolo, or go to New York, where other work awaited him. Marmion also asked D. Adelbert to send some of the money he was paid as an artist to Edermine priory. The money, which was quite a large sum, eventually arrived safely in Ireland. Owing to the war condition, Marmion was unable to acknowledge the receipt of the money from Brazil. However, after the war, when D. Adelbert made a short visit to Maredsous, Marmion called him out in front of the community in full Chapter, and publicly thanked him for providing the Edermine community with a large sum of money in 1915. Marmion's actual words were 'This is the man who kept the Edermine community alive during the war years. Thank you, Fr Adelbert!'

Marmion trusted his monks, gave them their heads, and did his best to see that they were all happy and fulfilled. There was no such thing in his mind as an odd man out.

Marmion loved his monks in a true Christian sense of the word. This is borne out especially in the case of those in poor health, or who had undergone an unfortunate experience. Such a case was that of D. Paul Damman, who died in 1919. The obituary notice which appeared in *Revue Liturgique et Monastique* is both moving and revealing. D. Paul was working in a Belgian parish when the invasion came in August 1914. He was captured and threatened with being shot. When he was released, he was a broken man, unable to settle down to monastic life. He spent much of the later war years in England and France, with Marmion's approval. Then in February 1919, word came that he was dying and wished to return to Maredsous. Although Marmion was absent in Rome at the time, he knew of D. Paul's situation and arranged that this monk would end his days among his confrères. D. Paul was brought back in a motor-car to Maredsous, and died there soon afterwards, only a shadow of his former self. He had not been abandoned by his abbot and community.

The intellectual influence of Maredsous under Marmion
Throughout his time as abbot, Marmion encouraged his monks in their different works and enterprises. He gave his special support to the three reviews which were regularly produced by the abbey: *Revue Bénédictine, Revue Liturgique et Monastique* and *Le Messager des Oblats*. These reviews provided an essential outlet for the writing talents of his monks, and they were well received by the general public, though obviously directed at different audiences.

However, Marmion wished for a more permanent and solid kind of publication, to be sponsored by Maredsous, which would bring some of the best religious writing to the general public. With this in mind, the monks of Maredsous began publishing a series called *Pax*, in collaboration with the French publishing firm Lethielleux, and the Belgian firm Desclée. Its aim was 'to make known the treasures of the church's literary heritage'. It consisted of works by Fathers of the Church, such as St Bernard and St Gregory the Great, also the writings of medieval mystics such as St Gertrude, and modern authors such as Bishop Hedley and Archbishop Ullathorne. The *Pax* collection also republished works such as those by D. Germain Morin, *L'idéal monastique et la vie chrétienne des premiers jours*, which had originally appeared in 1913. The series was an immediate success, and in time was to number about fifty volumes – a real treasury of Christian literature, put at the door of everyone in a readily acceptable format, and reasonably priced.

Pax was a post-war enterprise, and reached its highest peak of popularity towards the end of Marmion time as Abbot (1920-1923); it continued to expand and develop after his death. It was one of his most lasting legacies, and must be ranked alongside his own successful trilogy: *Christ, the Life of the Soul, Christ in His Mysteries,* and *Christ, the Life of the Monk.*

Marmion had certainly not sat back and enjoyed doing nothing during his thirteen years as Abbot of Maredsous. He had been a sound and diligent captain of his ship. He had maintained and upheld his crew and brought them all safely through troubled times. But he had also given them happy times, and this was only right, seeing that he was at all times a happy monk and a most encouraging abbot.

CHAPTER 13

Marmion:
Spiritual Writer *par excellence*

I. MARMION: SPIRITUAL WRITER AND GUIDE

Harmony and Mystery

It is not easy to classify Marmion's writings. They certainly are not purely devotional, neither are they purely theological. Cardinal Mercier, who was a personal friend of Marmion, wrote in the original Preface to *Christ the Life of the Soul*, that the book defied any narrow classification. He suggested that the best way to savour the book was 'to read and meditate upon it with the heart as well as with the head'. Perhaps the best way to approach Marmion is the spirit of those Viking warriors in Ireland long ago, who were travelling by boat along the River Shannon. Suddenly they heard in the distance the singing of monks. Their leader told the oarsmen to bring them close to the monastery so that they could listen to the *harmony of the monks*. And in the peace and silence of the monastery, they found something they had never dreamed of, another world, a new experience, a sense of mystery. Marmion felt he had a vocation to bring such a harmony into peoples' lives, primarily by explaining to them the mystery of Christ.

In Marmion's language, mystery means the hidden life of God, as lived by the Blessed Trinity. However, this mystery overflows into the lives of all men and women, through the liturgy, the sacraments, the reading of the bible, prayer and the practice of love or charity. More specifically, Marmion takes the mystery of Jesus Christ and shows how it touches people vitally and purposefully. His one aim in life was to *bring people to God and to bring God to people*.

Marmion's Message of Hope

Marmion knew from his long experience of dealing with people, that they were hungry for things of the spirit. As a young priest in Dublin, prior to his entering the abbey of Maredsous, he had served as chaplain to Mountjoy prison. Among the inmates were many hardened criminals – both men and women. He formed a rapport with some of them, and discovered how much they had become disillusioned with life. They spoke to him of the emptiness and nothingness of their existence. This was a time when such people were usually condemned to life imprisonment with no hope of ever attaining their freedom. Yet, Marmion succeeded in getting through to them and, in some few cases, brought hope and consolation, as well as faith in God's living mercy, into their lives. For the rest of his life, he was haunted by the memory of those unfortunates he had met in Mountjoy prison. Such an experience led Marmion to work out a *Theology of Hope*, convinced as he was that all men and women were called to a better destiny than this world could offer.

During his time as Abbot of Maredsous (1909-1923), his monastery became known as *The Parlour of Belgium*. People in every walk of life flocked to see him and ask for spiritual guidance. The world and human needs have not changed in the seventy or eighty years since Marmion lived. More and more people in our modern world are seeking peace of mind and soul through the practice of meditation. Some are turning to the Far East – to places like India and Malaysia – for inspiration, hoping to find there a wise man (a *guru* or *swami*) to give meaning to their lives. The problem with those who adopt the yoga or transcendental meditation techniques, is that they are often indulging in *self-seeking*. Marmion wished to put people on the road to *God-seeking*. For Marmion, all prayer and meditation had to lead to God, not to ourselves. He insisted that for Christians, Jesus Christ must be the centre and goal of all prayer, the only true way to union with God.

Marmion the Letter-writer
Marmion's spirituality cannot be fully appreciated without reference to his correspondence. Like many nineteenth century churchmen – one thinks immediately of John H. Newman – Marmion was a compulsive letter-writer. Some 1,800 letter have survived, of which about 300 were written in English. Written in an easy style and in a neat hand, they tell us much about his character and personality. One could say that the real Marmion is found in his letters, rather than in the trilogy. For those who have never read Marmion, it is recommended that they browse through the English Letters, before dipping into the trilogy.

Marmion had been brought up in Dublin, speaking English. Although his mother, Herminie Cordier, was French, English was his first language. He had undoubtedly learned some French from his mother, but it was only when he entered Maredsous in 1886, that he became fluent in that language. One will notice, therefore, some contrast between the language and style of the trilogy, which was originally written in French, and the English Letters. What emerges most clearly from the letters, is *Marmion's Irishness* – his sensitivity, his sense of humour, his overflowing heart. There is real affection, humanity and warmth in his letters, although he seldom strays far from the spiritual side of life.

Marmion had the ability to make friends, and to keep in touch with them, over a long number of years. Perhaps the best example of this, and certainly the most valuable from the historian's point of view, is his correspondence with Patrick Vincent Dwyer, a fellow student with Marmion in Clonliffe, and later bishop of Maitland, Australia. P. V. Dwyer was an Australian clerical student who had been sent by his bishop to Dublin to study for the priesthood. He was familiarly known to Marmion as 'Junk', because whenever he wanted a slice of bread at table he asked for a 'junk of bread', instead of a 'chunk of bread'. This ability to be familiar, and to make jokes, without hurting the feelings of the other party, was one of Marmion's strengths.

Later in life, he often called a correspondent by a pet-name, as in the case of a Carmelite sister of Louvain, Marie-Joseph Van Aerden, addressing her as 'Thecla', and signing himself 'Paul'. (Taking these names from the *Apocryphal Acts of Paul*). He gave the name 'Mousie' to a young English lady – Eveline Bax – because she found it difficult to make up her mind which religious congregation to join, and had tried four or five convents before making her final choice. However, despite these rather strange titles, the content of Marmion's spiritual letters has been published under the title *Union With God*. Work on the definitive edition of all Marmion's letters – in both French and English – is far advanced, and should be completed by 1998.

I. BACKGROUND TO MARMION'S SPIRITUALITY

Marmion a product of late nineteenth century

Marmion was born in the year 1858. By birth, upbringing and education, he was very much a product of the second half of the nineteenth century. It is agreed by most commentators that the Catholic Church in Western Europe, and in Ireland in particular, experienced a profound change in regard to religious practices between the years 1850 and 1900. As one writer has put it: 'From an austere and rather undemonstrative piety, there developed a form of worship, more accessible to the masses and giving greater scope to exterior devotions and emotional participation' (A. Draper). The man most responsible for this devotional revolution was Paul Cullen, Archbishop of Dublin from 1852-1878 (created cardinal in 1866). By a series of synods, both national or diocesan, as well as by encouraging parish missions or retreats, he encouraged many new devotions and religious practices, mostly of Roman origin: forty hours, perpetual adoration, novenas, blessed altars, benedictions of the Blessed Sacrament, stations of the Cross, jubilees, pilgrimages, processions, etc. Three particular devotions dominated the scene in Ireland in the latter half of the nineteenth century: to the Sacred Heart of Jesus, to the Eucharist, and to the Blessed Virgin.

Devotion to the Sacred Heart

In 1856, two years before Marmion's birth, Pius IX extended the feast of the Sacred Heart to the universal church. The Irish bishops consecrated Ireland to the Sacred Heart in 1873, just one year prior to Marmion's entering Clonliffe to study for the priesthood. It is interesting to note that Marmion recalls in one of his retreats, how his mother used to read to the family from a book called *The Imitation of the Sacred Heart*, written by a Fr Pierre Aernoudt, SJ. Evidently the book had greatly impressed him and he retained a personal devotion to the Sacred Heart throughout the rest of his life.

Devotion to the Sacred Heart was based essentially on an understanding of the love of Christ, and flowed from his heart. In practice, it was a means of associating oneself with the life and sufferings of Jesus. Religious congregations, such as the Sisters of the Sacred Heart, were founded to promote this particular devotion. Litanies of the Sacred Heart were introduced and went alongside such devotions as the Nine First Fridays, the Rosary and the Stations of the Cross. Marmion would have been brought up accepting such practices as normal and praiseworthy. Indeed, whenever possible, he made the Stations of the Cross, and recited the Rosary every day of his life. One could say that Marmion got his initiation into the life of Christ through these devotions. However, he later deepened his understanding of the Sacred Heart, and formed a synthesis of his thinking on the subject in his book *Christ in His Mysteries*. (See ch 19: 'The Heart of Christ'. One of the leading modern theologians, Hans Urs von Balthazar (+1988), has taken up this theme, and made it the subject of his book *The Heart of Christ*. It is interesting to note that Charles de Foucauld (1858-1916), a contemporary of Marmion, centred most of his personal devotion on the Sacred Heart, an image of which he had sewn on to his cloak.)

Devotion to the Eucharist
There was a very close link between devotion to the Sacred Heart and the eucharistic devotion. Jesus in the tabernacle, or in the host exposed in the monstrance at Benediction, provided a focal point for both religious and laity to unite themselves with Jesus. Religious congregations were established with the specific purpose of providing perpetual adoration of the Blessed Sacrament for their members. Marmion became personally associated with one such congregation, founded in Paris by Mother Adèle (Peter) Garnier, called the Adorers of Montmartre, who later moved to Tyburn Convent in London. Throughout the span of Marmion's life (1858-1923) adoration of the Blessed Sacrament was the most acceptable form of the contemplative life.

A number of factors helped to popularise devotion to the Blessed Sacrament. The first Eucharist Congress was held in Lille, France, in 1881. Such congresses, both national and international, have been held ever since. The result of all this was a considerable change of outlook and practice in regard to the reception of holy communion. Marmion, as a young boy, was allowed to receive communion only once a week, although he attended daily Mass with his parents. The movement towards more frequent communion was given a considerable boost in 1860, following the publication in France of a book by Mgr Ségur, called *La Très Sainte Communion*, which was immediately translated into most European languages, including English. In general, however, Catholics had to wait until the decrees of St Pius X in 1905 and 1910, advocating and encouraging daily reception of Communion, before it became an accepted norm.

All through his life, Marmion retained a deep devotion to the Blessed Eucharist. He wrote in his diary on 8 April 1887, when a novice in Maredsous: 'I had the happiness of spending nearly three hours before the Most Blessed Sacrament. I feel a great desire to love Jesus with my whole heart.' He saw the eucharist as the centre of the spiritual life of every Christian. There could be no real union with Christ for anyone who turned his back on the eucharist. He summed up his views on this matter in his book *Christ the Life of the Soul*: 'The Eucharist is, properly speaking, the sacrament of union, which nourishes and maintains the Divine life in us.' (Ch 7: 'The Eucharist Sacrifice')

Devotion to Mary
Although there has always been a deep devotion to Mary in the Catholic Church, the nineteenth century witnessed a tremendous increase in the practice of this devotion. Pius IX, in 1854, gave a lead, by declaring the dogma of the Immaculate Conception. However, it was Our Lady's appearance to Bernadette Soubirous at Lourdes, in 1858 (the year of Marmion's birth), which proved the real turning point. The first torchlight procession took place in Lourdes in 1872. Marmion had to wait until 1922 before making his first and only pilgrimage to this sacred shrine.

Marmion had a life-long devotion to Our Lady. During his early years, and indeed up to his entry into Maredsous in 1886, he always signed himself: *Joseph Marmion, E. de M. (Enfant de Marie – Child of Mary)*. Over and over again, in his retreats, as well as in his correspondence, he repeated the same message: 'We must be by Grace what Jesus is by nature, a child of God and a child of Mary. God will recognise as his true children only those who, like Jesus, are *children of Mary*.'

There was nothing ostentatious about Marmion's devotion to Mary, but rather he remained within the bounds of traditional Catholic devotion, relating everything about her to her Son. As a Benedictine monk, he was aware of the long tradition of liturgical prayer to Mary in monasteries. He loved to remind his listeners of the fact that most of the great cathedrals in England were built by Benedictine monks, and that they always had a special place behind the choir, called *The Lady Chapel*, where the Mass of Our Lady was sung every day. And when speaking of the rosary, Marmion liked to tell the story of St Alphonsus de Liguori, who during his last illness said the rosary almost without ceasing. One of the brethren remonstrated with St Alphonsus, saying: 'But you have already said your rosary. It is not necessary to repeat it ten times.' To which the saint replied: 'I must always say the rosary; my salvation depends on it.' On his own deathbed, Marmion asked those near him to join in saying the rosary, lingering over the words of the Hail Mary: 'Pray for us, sinners, now and at the hour of our death.'

III. THE MAIN SOURCES OF MARMION'S SPIRITUALITY

St Paul and St John

Marmion was by no means a biblical scholar. At the same time he had benefitted by following an excellent course in sacred scripture at the Propaganda Fide College in Rome during his student days. However, it must be said that he showed more interest in the New Testament than in the Old. He hardly ever quotes the Old Testament, apart from the Psalms, which he knew by heart. In the New Testament, he had a special love for the epistles of St Paul, and the gospel and epistles of St John. He saw sacred scripture, not through the eyes of an exegete or controversialist, but rather as a source or springboard for prayer and reflection.

The keynote of Marmion's spirituality is taken from chapter 1 of St Paul's epistle to the Ephesians, on the Divine Sonship. Over and over again Marmion says: 'If I were asked in what the spiritual life consists, I would answer: "Christ".' From his earliest days as a Benedictine monk in Maredsous, he began reflecting on the epistles of St Paul. He found the Pauline doctrine on the Divine Sonship most inspiring and helpful. A typical entrance in his diary, for 27 September 1887, is as follows: 'As I am the adopted son of God, I should try to imitate Jesus Christ perfectly, in his relations with the Holy Trinity.' In his book *Christ in His Mysteries*, Marmion tells us that 'the marvels of Divine Adoption are so great that human language cannot exhaust them. It is a wonderful thing that God should adopt us as his children.' It was above all from St Paul that Marmion got his Christ-centred view of the spiritual life.

At the same time, Marmion had a great love for St John the Evangelist. The trilogy and his letters are filled with quotations from St John. He found in St John, who reports so often the very words of Jesus, the secret to *Union with God*: 'If anyone love me,

my Father will love him, and we will take up our abode in him.'
(Jn 14:23) He was especially impressed with chapter 6 of St
John's gospel, and the words of Jesus: 'I am the bread of life. He
who comes to me will never be hungry; he who believes in me
will never be thirsty.' He found equal inspiration in the first
epistle of St John: 'We are sure that we live in union with God
and that he lives in union with us, because he has given us his
spirit.' (1 Jn 4:13) St John also provided him with confirmation of
his doctrine on Divine Sonship: 'See how much the father has
loved us! His love is so great that we are called God's children –
and so, in fact, we are.' (1 Jn 3:1) *Christ the Life of the Soul* can be
called a commentary on St John's gospel and epistles.

The Liturgy
Marmion, as a Benedictine monk, spent a great deal of his time
in choir, taking part in the Divine Office. There is no doubt that
his inner spiritual life, as well as his teaching, owed much to the
liturgy. He liked to refer to the Divine Office as 'a real granary
prepared by God himself', and never tired of insisting on the im-
portance of time spent in choir for the religious man or woman:
'When we faithfully apply ourselves to the recitation of the
Divine Office, the Holy Spirit gives us gradually a deep knowledge of the perfection of God and of the mysteries of Christ.'
(Quoted by I. Ryelandt, in *American Benedictine Review*, Spring
1961, p. 14) He wrote to his friend, P. V. Dwyer, in 1888: 'The
chief object of our congregation is to carry out the sacred liturgy
and the chant of the church. *I had no idea that such riches and beauty
were contained in the Divine Office.*' Later, he put these thoughts
into his conferences, which, when gathered together, formed the
basis for *Christ in His Mysteries*.

Marmion's life coincided with a very considerable renewal and
flowering of liturgical studies, especially in France, where Dom
Guéranger, the Abbot of Solesmes, produced a monumental
work called *The Liturgical Year*, the first nine volumes of which
appeared between 1841 and 1865. Marmion makes several references to Guéranger's masterpiece and undoubtedly found it a
source for his own reflections. Soon after he was elected Abbot,
Marmion held a Liturgical Congress (in 1912) in Maredsous and,
in his inauguration address, used the phrase the *liturgical movement*. He must have been one of the first people to do so.

A careful reading of Marmion's trilogy will open up for us new
liturgical horizons. If Marmion sees Christ as the heart of the

liturgy, he goes on to assure us that 'the Mass is the heart of the church's worship, if not the centre of all religion'. At the same time, he warns us against externalising our religion too much: 'All true worship is *interior*. The perfection of the ceremonies, the beauty of the music and the liturgical ornaments, the harmony of the ritual, serve only as rungs of a ladder, whereby the soul is led from the visible world to the contemplation of the invisible, supernatural realities.' (*C. H. M.* 2, 2)

St Thomas Aquinas, Mgr Gay and St Francis de Sales

Marmion puts St Thomas Aquinas, the great Dominican theologian and doctor of the church, at the top of his list of authorities, after the Bible and the Rule of St Benedict. He had studied the *Summa* of St Thomas in Rome, under Professor Satolli, and never ceased to fall back on this source as a sure guide to Catholic thought.

One of Marmion's favourite ascetical writers was Mgr Charles Gay (1815-1880), a French priest-theologian, who later became a bishop. Someone has said that 'in their character, doctrinal outlook, theological formation and spirituality, Marmion and Gay have much in common. One could almost say that they were kindred spirits, though they had never met' (*Dict. de Spirit*, VI, co. 159-171). Mgr Gay's writings were originally given as conferences to different groups of religious women – especially the Carmelites. In both origin and content, they have very much in common with Marmion's own publications. Gay introduced his two volumes, entitled *Elevations on the Life and Doctrine of Jesus Christ*, with these words: 'This book was born *in prayer and indeed from prayer*. If you want to get the most out of it, you should read it in the same spirit in which it was composed, that is by praying, or at least with the intention of advancing in the science (art) of prayer' (Preface to French edition, p. XXVII).

The third great influence on Marmion's spiritual formation was St Francis de Sales (1567-1622), whose two classical works: *Treatise on the Love of God* and *Introduction to the Devout Life*, were read and re-read by Marmion throughout his life. Their common bond was evident in their missionary zeal and endeavour to bring God into the lives of all Christians. Marmion acknowledged his debt to St Francis de Sales in the following words: 'I love him more and more, and as I advance in age, my esteem for him continues to grow' (*Mélanges Marmion*, p. 68). On another occasion, he confided to a friend: 'I have read lately Book IX of the *Treatise on the Love of God* by St Francis de Sales. His ideas co-incide with mine in everything' (Quoted by I. Ryelandt, *A. B. R.*, Spring 1951, p. 30). The key words in the ascetical and doctrinal teaching of both men were: moderation and discretion.

IV. PROBLEMS FOR TODAY'S READERS OF MARMION

The composition of the Marmion Trilogy

Marmion's three books were not composed by Dom Marmion himself with a view to publication. The work was done by one of his monks, Dom Raymond Thibaut, based on long and short-hand notes taken during conferences given by Marmion, and also from manuscript notes made by Marmion himself. Most, if not all, the words are Marmion's and he was able in each case to control, approve or amend some of the texts prepared by Thibaut. However, it must be said that the text lacks the personal touch. It is difficult sometimes to see the real Marmion in these volumes. Above all, the trilogy lacks the stories and anecdotes with which Marmion always illustrated his conferences. Those who took down the words of Marmion, for some strange reason omitted his stories. Perhaps these good stenographers were over-anxious to get the spiritual message correct, and took a breather whenever Marmion told a story. More's the pity! We have evidence of those who attended his conferences, that he always garnished them with stories. Marmion was, by nature, a jovial person and a good storyteller.

Spiritual reading in the Twenty-First Century

It seems that few people today have time or inclination for serious reading of any kind. How different things were in Marmion's day, when spiritual treatises often ran to two or three volumes. It is hard to imagine how the arrival of a preacher or retreat-giver was a major event in the lives of a religious com-munity or parish. People were overjoyed to welcome someone who would help them pass the time of day. Retreat givers such as Marmion were greatly appreciated and respected. When his books were published, they read them from cover to cover with relish. However, Marmion's world has passed away. Yet here we are, on the threshold of the twenty-first century, trying to read and understand him. Marmion has too many rivals in our age of radio, television, sporting events, and the internet. How does Marmion fit into such a way of life? The only sensible advice one can give in regard to reading Marmion today, is to take a chapter or less at a time. His books do not lend themselves to concentrated reading – at least for the general reader. If one looks for a liturgical uplift, then the relevant chapters in *Christ in His Mysteries* will help, and even satisfy us. If one is seeking help in one's prayer-life, the chapters on prayer in *Christ the Life of the Soul* or *Christ the Ideal of the Monk,* should be read. The present writer has experienced many people who continue to find inspiration in reading Marmion. It is a fact that Marmion helped form several generations of priests, religious and laity, between the years 1920 and 1960. He cannot possibly have gone out-of-date, or out-of-fashion, so quickly and so irrevocably. There is no shortcut to entering on the inner spiritual world of Marmion. The main thing is to set out on the road, with Marmion in our bag. That way, we shall surely arrive at the end of our life's journey, much enriched and much enlightened.